1

IMMERSED - The Definitive Guide to Sous Vide Cooking

Published by:
PolyScience®
A division of Preston Industries
6600 West Touhy Avenue
Niles, IL 60714-4588
USA

PolyScience is a registered trademark of Preston Industries Inc.

ANTI-GRIDDLE, THE SMOKING GUN, SOUS VIDE, SOUS VIDE PROFESSIONAL, SOUS VIDE TOOLBOX are trademarks of Breville Pty Ltd.

On July 1st, 2014 Breville (Australia) Pty. Ltd. and Preston Industries Inc. (PolyScience) announced a strategic alliance whereby Breville would acquire the global distribution rights for the current and future PolyScience Culinary products in both the consumer and commercial channels.

Thanks to David Arnold at CookingIssues.com for providing imagery.

Food photography courtesy of David Pietranczyk.

IMMERSED

The Definitive Guide
To Sous Vide Cooking

By Philip Preston

TABLE OF CONTENTS

FOREWORD

WHAT IS SOUS VIDE? 8-9

MY STORY WITH SOUS VIDE 10-17

BENEFITS OF SOUS VIDE 18

SOUS VIDE MAKES COOKING EGGS EASY 19

A BRIEF HISTORY OF SOUS VIDE 20-21

ESSENTIALS OF SOUS VIDE 22-23

VARYING TIME & TEMPERATURE 24

SOUS VIDE TOOLBOX™ 25

EQUIPMENT OVERVIEW 26-27

ANATOMY OF A CIRCULATOR 28

CONTRIBUTION FROM BRUNO GOUSSAULT 30-31

STEP BY STEP SOUS VIDE SUCCESS 32-33

RECIPES

INTRODUCTION 34-35

BREAKFAST 36

HOLLANDAISE SAUCE 38-39

EGGS BENEDICT 40-41

FRENCH TOAST & BOURBON-INFUSED PEACHES 42-43

YOGURT & BLUEBERRY COMPOTE 44-45

GRANOLA 45

LUNCH 46

BUFFALO CHICKEN WINGS WITH SMOKED RANCH DRESSING ... 48-49

MAC & CHEESE WITH GARLIC BREAD CRUMBS 50-51

CARNE ASADA, VACUUM-PICKLED ESCEBECHE & SMOKED SALSA ROJA ... 52-55

POACHED RHUBARB 56

CAULIFLOWER SOUP 56

DIVER SCALLOPS 58-59

RED & GOLD BEETS 60

LOBSTER ROLL 61

DINNER _____ 62

    NEW YORK STRIP STEAK, MASHED YUKON GOLD POTATOES & ASPARAGUS _____ 64-67
    CORN SOUP WITH BACON-SHALLOT JAM _____ 68-69
    72-HOUR SHORT RIBS, CUMIN BUTTER CARROTS & BRUSSELS SPROUTS _____ 70-72
    RIB RUB & MUSTARD BARBECUE SAUCE _____ 73
    BABY BACK RIBS WITH CORN ON THE COB _____ 74-75
    POACHED SALMON, CELERY ROOT & CANNELLINI BEAN SOUP _____ 76-79
    PHILIP'S THANKSGIVING DARK & WHITE MEAT, SPICED DUCK FAT & SMASHED SWEET POTATOES _____ 80-82
    DOUBLE-CUT PORK CHOPS & CREAMY POLENTA WITH WILD MUSHROOMS _____ 83-85
    DUCK CONFIT _____ 86-87
    DUCK BREAST & SAFFRON ISRAELI COUSCOUS WITH RAISINS & EDAMAME _____ 88-89
    DAVE'S BUTTERMILK FRIED CHICKEN WITH HERB INFUSED HONEY _____ 90-91
    CHATEAUBRIAND FOR TWO _____ 92-93
    RACK OF LAMB WITH ARTICHOKES BY BRUNO GOUSSAULT _____ 94-95

DESSERT _____ 96

    COCONUT ICE CREAM BY JOHNNY IUZZINI _____ 98
    AERATED COCONUT PASSION CURD BY JOHNNY IUZZINI _____ 99
    BANANA CREAM PIE WITH TOASTED COCONUT _____ 100-101
    VANILLA BEAN ICE CREAM WITH MALTED CARAMEL SAUCE AND SPICE POACHED APPLES _____ 102-103
    CLASSIC POUND CAKE WITH LEMON CURD _____ 104-105

COCKTAILS _____ 106

    GLÖGG _____ 108
    PEACH-INFUSED GIN _____ 109
    PEACH GIN & TONIC _____ 109
    GRAPEFRUIT FOAM _____ 110
    GINGER-CITRUS MOCKTAIL _____ 111
    GINGER-LIME SODA BASE _____ 111
    MANHATTAN WITH SOUS VIDE BITTERS _____ 112-113
    PSC BITTERS BATCH 01 _____ 112-113
    APPLE-INFUSED GIN _____ 114
    APPLE-ROSEMARY MARTINI _____ 114
    THE HOST _____ 115

TECHNICAL REFERENCE _____ 116-123

ACKNOWLEDGEMENTS _____ 124-125

FOREWARD

Having employed sous vide cooking techniques in my own kitchen for more than a decade, I can provide you with countless reasons why you should consider adding sous vide to your culinary repertoire.

But for me, the simplest reason may also be the most compelling: Whether you're working in a professional kitchen or simply preparing meals at your home, sous vide will make you a better cook — in whatever way you choose to define that term.

Sous vide provides you with unprecedented control over cooking temperatures, which allows you to prepare your favorite meals, time and again, with little fear of failure. It tenderizes foods, imbues them with more pronounced and nuanced flavors as well as yields succulent textures that you simply can't achieve by any other method. It also happens to take much of the stress out of cooking — freeing up valuable time for you to be more creative, to multi-task in the kitchen or simply spend extra time with your family and friends.

I developed this cookbook in hopes of helping you experience many of the same bursts of excitement and creativity that I've encountered while working with sous vide — all without having to endure any of the setbacks and frustrations I had to overcome during my journey.

When I started working with sous vide, there was a dearth of reference materials on the subject. Today, research on sous vide is amassing, not only in regards to calibrating cooking temperatures and prep times but also in proving just how safe sous vide cooking can truly be.

Combining this research with my own experiences, I've attempted to create a cookbook that simply and succinctly lays out all the most critical information and best practices you need to start cooking sous vide safely and efficiently.

If you're looking for mere sustenance, this is not the cookbook for you. I realize that a lot of people are content with buying a box of store-bought pancake mix, whipping it up and calling it a day, but I happen to enjoy the entire process of cooking.

The truth of the matter is, making well-prepared meals for the ones I love gives me great personal pleasure. I love tinkering with ways of forging new flavor combinations and then layering them together in a way that shows I've put a great deal of thought and effort into each preparation. And I love the artistry of plating a meal, creating dishes that are as appealing to the eyes as they are pleasing to the palate.

And thus, sous vide has allowed me to prepare more flavorful, healthier, and more memorable meals than I ever could before. It's expanded my comfort zone, gracing me with a newfound confidence that has allowed me to expand my culinary horizons in new and unexpected ways.

Should you welcome sous vide into your own kitchen, I am confident that it will do the same — and much, much more — for you and yours as well.

Philip Preston

WHAT IS SOUS VIDE?

WHAT'S IN A NAME?

The term "sous vide," which translates from the French as "under vacuum," was coined because its early proponents in France saw vacuum-sealing as an essential part of the process. Today, as sous vide has evolved and become better understood, the term "precise temperature cooking" might be a better descriptor for the process, as vacuum packing is not always necessary. Regardless of which name you choose to use, sous vide is easy to learn, offering chefs a new technique to add to their culinary repertoires that artfully complements traditional cooking methods.

THE SOUS VIDE CONCEPT IS SIMPLE.

Food is packaged in sealable plastic pouches or in other food-safe containers. These packages are then submerged in circulating water baths that are warmed to specific temperatures by mechanical heaters. Much like setting your thermostat at home, you can assign a desired temperature for the water and then maintain that same temperature throughout the cooking process. Removing as much air as possible from the containers guarantees that the food remains completely submerged in the water, thus cooking your food evenly from all sides. Consequently, plastic pouches sealed by vacuum-sealing devices (like those used to store leftovers in the freezer) remain the most popular packaging method, even as inroads continue to be made by other newer techniques and equipment.

TEMPERATURE CONTROL IS THE KEY TO KITCHEN SUCCESS.

Cooking is ultimately about preparing food with heat. The more control you have over heat, the more control you have over the quality of your cooking. Sous vide is simply a means of precisely controlling the temperature of your food. When cooking sous vide, meals are sealed in food-safe pouches and heated in water baths at gentle temperatures until the desired level of doneness is achieved. Virtually no other cooking method provides more control, allowing you to consistently deliver perfectly cooked foods and preparations, time after time, with unprecedented regularity.

MY STORY WITH SOUS VIDE

In 2005, Matthias Merges, the longtime executive chef at *Charlie Trotter's* restaurant in Chicago, handed me a gift — a vacuum-sealed plastic pouch filled with seafood — that ultimately changed my life.

Matthias had invited me into his kitchen to discuss his latest culinary pursuit: sous vide cooking. At the time, sous vide was an under-appreciated cooking technique in the United States. Sous vide called for meats, seafood, sauces and vegetables to be vacuum-sealed in an airtight plastic pouch and then gently warmed in a temperature-controlled water bath.

When properly executed, the sous vide method provides an unprecedented level of control over the internal temperatures of ingredients. Set a thermostat on a typical oven and you can expect its internal heat to fluctuate 10 degrees above or below your preferred temperature.

Set that same temperature in a proper immersion circulator — the name for the compact Jacuzzi-like water baths used in sous vide cooking — and the temperature will never fluctuate more than one-tenth of a degree from your target.

Matthias had invited me to Charlie Trotter's because my company, PolyScience®, is in the business of making immersion circulators for commercial and scientific companies. We hit it off from the start. He talked about cooking and the culinary arts. I talked about thermodynamics and proper temperature control. And at the end of our meeting, Matthias handed me a vacuum-sealed pouch of Tasmanian sea trout for me to cook sous vide at home.

At the time, my wife and I had never eaten at Charlie Trotter's, so the pouch felt like a free four-star carry-out meal. I raced home, dropped the bag into my immersion circulator, set the temperature and then waited 25 minutes for our meal to be done.

Initially, I was worried. As I stared down at our beautiful trout, I wondered if I had done something wrong. It all felt too easy. How, I wondered, could I have achieved this stunning result by doing so little?

I had never, in all my years of cooking, encountered a texture quite like that filet of sous vide sea trout. It was buttery and soft, yet brimming with deep, rich flavors that tasted like they'd been infused into every morsel of the fish.

The sous vide process seemed to blend together the best elements of my favorite culinary techniques: the richness of a slow braise, the delicacy of cooking *en papillote* and the grace of a delicate poach.

After the meal, I felt a surge of excitement. The idea of cooking sous vide had energized two very disparate parts of my personality: my inner chef and my inner engineer. It was science and art. Taste and technology. My own personal yin and yang.

I felt both invigorated and satiated, the hallmarks of any great meal. I didn't know quite what to do next. All I knew was that I felt an immediate connection to this strange cooking process called sous vide — and was committed to bringing the experience to as many homes and restaurants across the country as I could.

My mother is an artist, the chef and photographer of the family. My father was an inventor, a man of science and innovation. Over the years, sous vide allows me to honor them both in my own way.

At a cooking demonstration with my mother, who inspired my love of cooking and the culinary arts.

Cooking has always been an essential element of my life. I spent many unforgettable summers with my grandparents on the Belgian coast. We would take our fishing nets out to the beach and bring back tiny shrimp. Our *bonne maman* would spend the afternoon meticulously peeling away their tiny iridescent shells. She folded the baby shrimp into her own homemade mayonnaise and then gently lined the interior of a cored tomato with the mix, creating one of my all-time favorite meals.

Like so many Europeans who endured the horrors of Nazi occupation, my family's appreciation for good food was deep and almost reverential, treating each ingredient with great care and consideration. My mother cooked with a similar soulfulness here in the United States. She enjoyed the ritual of eating, the act of bringing all of us together to enjoy each other's company, which reminded us to give thanks for our good fortune and the richness of our heritage.

I am an inventor and a cook, a unique combination of logic and artistry that stems from the eclectic interests of my mother and father.

In an era dominated by canned food and TV dinners, my mother held strong to her Belgian roots. She prepared everything from scratch, including her carbonnade flamande, a Belgian stew. Thanks to my mom, I didn't know what store-bought mayonnaise tasted like until I left home — and still crave the real stuff whenever I eat French fries.

But my fondest memories involve her famous pain d'almonde, simple yet delicious cookies that she loved to make until she was well into her 80s and made available to anyone passing through her kitchen. Whenever I returned home from school, I would be greeted by the smell of cinnamon and the sound of my mom calling out in her high sing-song French accent, "I have something good for you to eat!"

It was an incredibly warm and reassuring way to grow up; it's a blessing to know that people you love are willing to take the time and energy to make you home-cooked meals and delicious food. I'm eternally grateful and carry on the same traditions with my own family.

My earliest attempts at cooking came as a teenager, after I bought my first kitchen gadget: a hand-crank ice cream maker. I whipped up every ice cream flavor you can imagine. I quickly learned that it's difficult to make sugar, cream and eggs taste bad with the right equipment and dedication. Countless culinary experiments followed, during which I learned the importance of control. For me, it was a pure cause-and-effect relationship. The more effectively I could regulate the temperatures of the food I was cooking, the more successful the result.

Most young boys think their dad is brilliant. But now, as I've grown up and become a father myself, I know that my dad truly was an amazing man.

How, I wondered, could I gain more control over the cooking process? How could I regulate the temperatures with more precision and accuracy? How could I make the cooking process more simple yet flavorful?

Ironic, I guess, considering that I would find the answers to those very questions in my dad's own laboratory.

My father was always interested in a vast array of technologies and was a pioneer in the field of gas chromatography.

He encouraged me to tinker from an early age. When I was young, he helped me transform a broken-down old lawn mower into my very own go-kart, complete with a rickety two-by-four for a seat. I learned the importance of applying a scientific approach to a given problem — and to always be as efficient in my work as possible.

As a professor of chemical engineering, my father built several interconnected businesses. He created chemical reference standards that helped companies identify unknown chemicals. He founded the *Journal of Chromatographic Science* and the *Journal of Analytical Toxicology*. As a lover of photography, he also started *Photo Techniques*, a highly respected photography magazine, which was often filled with my mom's stunning pictures.

When I was 8 years old, he founded PolyScience®, a company dedicated to creating innovative American-made lab equipment. Our whole family worked, in our own way, for the company. My mother translated for European customers; my brothers sold equipment; my sister created promotional materials. I repaired equipment and ran the printing press. We all swept the floor.

As a young man, I took French cooking classes in the evening, wanting to re-create the food I had growing up.

My dad instilled in each of us a deep pride and appreciation for hard work. We were together as a family and my mother's home cooking would always be waiting for us at the end of the day.

I worked on a race-car pit crew, but always found myself gravitating back to the family company. So in 1982, I returned home, and took a full time position at PolyScience®.

The core PolyScience® products we developed back then — and continue to develop today — are designed to carefully control liquid temperatures for a variety of commercial, industrial and medical environments, including hospitals, electron microscopy labs and viscosity testing labs.

In 1986, our team of brilliant engineers helped us expand our business by creating equipment that assisted researchers and forensic specialists in analyzing DNA fragments, including O.J. Simpson's famous glove during his murder trial in the

mid-1990s. But we'd never sold one of our devices to a chef until I received that fateful call from Matthias Merges in 2005.

Those meetings with Matthias proved to be a turning point, not only in my life as a chef but in my professional career as well. Months after my first foray into sous vide cooking, I was contacted by the innovative chef and restaurateur Wylie Dufresne of the iconic *wd~50* in New York. Wylie had been invited to compete on the Food Network's *Iron Chef America* TV show and needed circulators for the challenge.

I quickly provided them and later watched Wylie pull a perfectly cooked tilapia creation from one of our devices during the show. Word quickly spread throughout the culinary world, and soon a market for used immersion circulators began to form on eBay.

Knowing that chefs shouldn't be using circulators that had been previously used in scientific labs, I developed a new circulator designed especially for the kitchen, wrapping its critical pump and heaters with a stainless-steel cage to help it withstand the rigors of restaurant life.

In the meantime, I began practicing sous vide cooking in my own kitchen — often with encouraging results. When I cooked skirt steaks sous vide and then finished them on the grill, they became as tender as a filet mignon yet retained their rich umami flavor. And by throwing my baby back ribs into a circulator, I could break down their connective tissues with ease, creating incredibly flavorful but tender ribs.

Here I am with my father, Seaton T. Preston Jr., examining an example of the first disposable camera at the 1986 Photo Marketing Association Show.

The Anti-Griddle® can be used to almost instantaneously create frozen treats like these made by chef Grant Achatz.

Typically, 60 minutes before Thanksgiving dinner is rush hour in any kitchen. When you're trying to orchestrate so many things and get them all on the table at the same time, you lose the ability to enjoy the moment. Not anymore. As I talked with my family, I was stress-free, knowing that my mashed potatoes wouldn't burn and that my turkey had no chance of overcooking.

And thus sous vide was providing me a great, unforeseen blessing. It was allowing me to cook a memorable meal for my family without having to sacrifice our time together. It was a moment to be thankful for — and an experience I hope this cookbook will grant you and your family as well.

Luckily, things just kept getting better professionally. One day, a brilliant young chef named Grant Achatz and his business partner, Nick Kokonas, asked to meet me at our factory in Niles, just outside of Chicago. At the time, Grant was developing his revolutionary recipes in Nick's home kitchen, creating the foundation for their ground-breaking restaurant *Alinea*.

My first meeting with Grant gave me the inspiration to create another invention. Seeing that our technology could raise, lower and control temperature within one one-hundredth of a degree, he asked if we could create a special "cold plate" for freezing food in a unique way.

Normally when you put something in a freezer, cold air blasts over an ingredient in all directions, freezing it from the outside in. Grant wanted a unidirectional cold plate that would simply freeze from the bottom up, allowing him to crystallize the base of an ingredient or sauce while allowing its top to stay in a liquid-like or unfrozen form.

A few months later, we delivered our invention, the Anti-Griddle®, which would go on to win the Food Network's 2007 Tasty Technology Award. Not only has Grant used the Anti-Griddle® to amazing effect at his restaurants, creating partially frozen dollops of sour cream topped with shreds of salmon, caterers and bartenders from around the country have embraced the device as well.

At that point, I was on a creative roll, both personally and professionally.

My wife and I had our first baby, and amidst the happy delirium and sleep deprivation, I had an epiphany at an office-supply store. I came across one of those battery-powered, hand-held vacuum cleaners that suck up and remove dust from keyboards and quickly realized I could tweak the device to make the first widely accessible cold smoker for food.

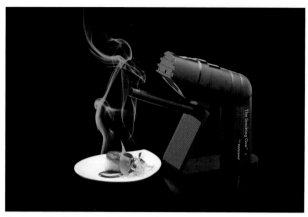

I originally developed The Smoking Gun® to enhance sous vide prepared foods but discovered that it does much more.

I brought one home and created a prototype for my new smoker on my kitchen counter. Modeling the design after an old-fashioned gentleman's pipe, I created a chamber at the top where I could stuff smoke-worthy ingredients — like tea, wood or even spices. Once those elements were burned, smoky flavors puffed out of the front of the device, allowing chefs to infuse their meals with deeply rich aromas.

The Smoking Gun® was born. Grant Achatz at *Alinea* uses it to pump the aroma of smoked autumn leaves over one of his signature dishes. And I crushed up a cigar and piped the smoke over a Manhattan, creating my own "Smoky Manhattan" cocktail. The possibilities for its use remain endless.

Sensing an increased demand for our culinary products, I pulled together a small, tight-knit team of professionals to create a culinary division within PolyScience®, which continues to sell our devices to amateur and professional chefs all around the world.

It's been an amazing ride. I've been fortunate to work with some of the most brilliant chefs and scientists.

My dream of expanding the use of sous vide into home kitchens continues with the publication of this book.

I know I am on the right track, in part because of what we accomplished at my brother's wedding reception in 2011, which might mark the high point of my work as a sous vide cook.

I wanted to give my brother and his wife an unforgettable celebration. Family was coming in from all over the country, along with 200 guests, and I needed to create and serve a meal in the middle of a remote field in northern Wisconsin.

How can you cook a great meal for 200 people in the middle of the woods with only six electrical outlets at your disposal? I now had a secret weapon: my sous vide equipment and experience.

To get the job done, I prepared the duck confit and tenderloin sous vide ahead of time, packed them up on the big day and then methodically finished the beef on the grill, the duck in a turkey fryer and a batch of cumin-buttered carrots in four of my immersion circulators.

I'm proud to say the meal went precisely as planned: crispy duck, juicy medium-rare slices of tenderloin and buttery-rich carrots.

One of my brother's guests came up to me and said, "This isn't the best wedding food I've ever had; this might be the best food I've ever eaten, period." I was able to provide our close friends and family a well-cooked meal and a dining experience that we will never ever forget.

I sincerely hope this book creates the same opportunity for you and yours, one delicious sous vide meal at a time.

Chef Grant Achatz using an Anti-Griddle® to make his interpretation of Starburst candies at the 2009 National Restaurant Show.

SOUS VIDE INSIGHTS

by Grant Achatz

Chef & Owner of Alinea, Next, and The Aviary

Back when I was at Trio in Evanston, our budgets were extremely thin. We would go to Costco and get a tiny little food saver, a vacuum compressor, to cryovac food because we couldn't afford anything else. So we just got this hundred-dollar one, but it came with a 30-day warranty. And inevitably within 30 days, it would break and one of the chefs would have to take it back to Costco and get a new one for free. That's how we started doing sous vide at Trio.

My relationship with Philip was serendipitous. He was obviously super into food. He had made friends with chef Matthias Merges at Trotter's. And I think, at some point, Matthias might have said to Philip, "You should probably go see this guy at Trio. He's doing some weird, cool stuff. You guys might get along really well."

So Philip and I hooked up. I went out to his place, and he was showing me what he could do, and I just started asking him questions. I didn't think anything would come of it, but I said to him, "We've all worked on a flattop, a French cooking flattop that gets to 500° F. Can we make one that gets to negative 500 degrees?" And all of a sudden, the relationship between Philip and I changed in the most positive way because we were challenging each other. I had the culinary vision, and he had the technological vision to make these Frankenstein things happen. And within a couple weeks, he came to me and said, "I have what I think we should call 'the Anti-Griddle.'"

I went out to Niles, and sure enough, we were throwing things on a stainless steel plate and they're freezing. And then we went on and on: smoking gun and distillation machines and so on.

The coolest thing is that Philip is a foodie. He enjoys the experience of eating, but he's also a scientist, so he just finds an immense amount of enjoyment in bridging those two worlds, in saying, "I'm going to help chefs do something that normally they would never be able to accomplish because I know science, but I can also speak their language and figure what they want in terms of their food." And that's why he and I hit it off, and we've been friends ever since.

BENEFITS OF SOUS VIDE

The benefits of sous vide are many, and each chef finds their own personal reasons for utilizing the technique. The primary benefit of sous vide is its ability to precisely control the cooking temperature of food, which yields consistent perfection in terms of texture and doneness. You will never have to worry about overcooking or undercooking anything ever again. The secondary benefit is the intensity of flavors that are created as a result of the ingredients being vacuum-sealed before cooking. As a result, sous vide provides both professional chefs and home chefs unparalleled flexibility and freedom to produce delicious creations while drastically reducing the inherent stresses of their kitchens.

PRECISE CONTROL

Temperature impacts all aspects of the cooking process, including the texture, aroma, color and taste of your food. Altering cooking temperatures by the subtle difference of just one degree can be the difference between a sumptuous meal and an overcooked or undercooked disaster. The texture and flavor of an egg can vary considerably when cooked at different temperatures, as illustrated in the chart to the right. Sous vide cooking allows you to easily control temperatures within an amazing 0.1°F/0.07°C. Moreover, once the desired internal temperature of the food is reached, sous vide cooking allows you the ability to leave your food in the bath for an extended time without overcooking it.

EFFICIENCY

- Makes sinewy secondary cuts of meat as tender as more expensive cuts.

- Delivers significant energy savings based on greater cooking efficiencies and reduced ventilation needs.

- Allows meals to be partially cooked ahead of time, easing the pressures of workday meals and dinner parties.

CONVENIENCE

- Provides perfect portion control.

- Requires minimal training.

- Provides flexible storage and cooking options that can be tailored to your exact needs and budget.

TIME MANAGEMENT

- Enjoy perfect results without the stress of perfect timing.

MASTERY

- Extends holding times and maintains exact doneness even for delicate foods, such as fish and lobster.

- Practically eliminates the risk of overcooking.

- Produces moist and tender textures. Captures and intensifies flavors.

- The combination of sous vide with searing, roasting and other more traditional cooking methods produces truly amazing results that can't be replicated by any other single technique.

- Makes marinating meat and seafood as well as macerating fruits and vegetables fast and easy.

- Retains nutrients, vibrant colors and aromas.

- Allows for easy reheating and holds foods at serving temperatures without moisture loss or risk of burning.

SOUS VIDE MAKES COOKING EGGS EASY

Countless breakfast offerings rely on eggs — and we all like our eggs prepared in a specific way — the egg chart below provided by Dave Arnold of CookingIssues.com is designed to help you determine exactly how long and at what temperature to cook your eggs in order to achieve your own definition of perfection.

It should be noted that egg yolks solidify at a lower temperature than egg whites. Most people don't realize this as they poach eggs in boiling water. Using the sous vide method, the yolks are always firmer than the whites.

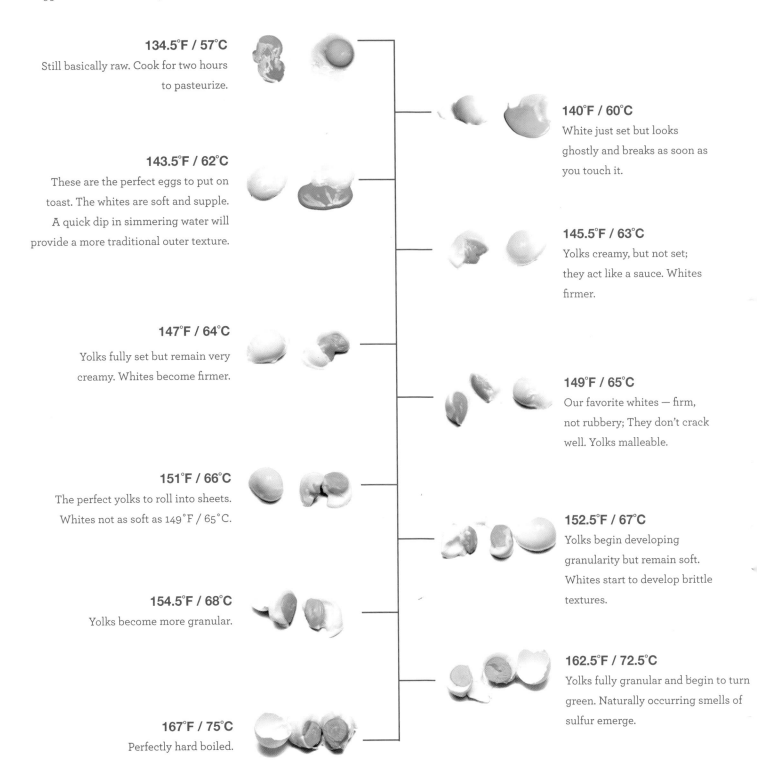

134.5°F / 57°C

Still basically raw. Cook for two hours to pasteurize.

140°F / 60°C

White just set but looks ghostly and breaks as soon as you touch it.

143.5°F / 62°C

These are the perfect eggs to put on toast. The whites are soft and supple. A quick dip in simmering water will provide a more traditional outer texture.

145.5°F / 63°C

Yolks creamy, but not set; they act like a sauce. Whites firmer.

147°F / 64°C

Yolks fully set but remain very creamy. Whites become firmer.

149°F / 65°C

Our favorite whites — firm, not rubbery; They don't crack well. Yolks malleable.

151°F / 66°C

The perfect yolks to roll into sheets. Whites not as soft as 149°F / 65°C.

152.5°F / 67°C

Yolks begin developing granularity but remain soft. Whites start to develop brittle textures.

154.5°F / 68°C

Yolks become more granular.

162.5°F / 72.5°C

Yolks fully granular and begin to turn green. Naturally occurring smells of sulfur emerge.

167°F / 75°C

Perfectly hard boiled.

A BRIEF HISTORY OF SOUS VIDE

Although sous vide may be a relatively new culinary technique, the idea of slowly and carefully cooking ingredients in an envelope of heat has a long, storied history. In some cultures, chefs have been wrapping meats, seafood and vegetables in wet, aromatic leaves for generations, burying them among warm rocks as a means of tenderization and a way of absorbing fragrant aromas.

Sous vide is simply another form of "low and slow" cooking. When we barbecue, we seal our steaks and brats in a cloud of smoke. When we braise, we immerse our pot roasts and short ribs in a liquid bath. And when we use a pressure cooker, we are steaming our vegetable medleys in a pressurized dome of hot air.

The development of contemporary sous vide cooking can be largely attributed to the efforts of two French culinary innovators working separately on the same idea during the early 1970s. Chef George Pralus originally employed sous vide as a means of preparing foie gras, hoping to delicately warm the precious delicacy in a way that preserved flavor while retaining its moisture and weight.

On the other hand, Bruno Goussault set out to study sous vide's broader applications as a cooking technique and remains highly involved in the field as a chef and scientist at CREA, The Culinary Research and Education Academy, as well as Cuisine Solutions, Inc., a supplier of sous vide-prepared foods. We're proud to showcase some of his thought-provoking insights on pages 30-31.

Sous vide has survived the test of time and is growing in popularity because it's both fun and forgiving — and because it intensifies flavors while yielding mouthwateringly supple textures. Though sous vide is not yet an everyday technique for the home chef, it is increasingly practiced today in a wide range of food-service operations, from fine-dining restaurants and airplanes to the dining halls of the U.S. military. Given the increasing ubiquity of the technique, it is highly likely that you've enjoyed meals cooked sous vide without even knowing it.

Luckily, today's cutting-edge technologies allow you to employ sous vide cooking techniques in your own kitchen, providing you the ability to prepare meals with the same depth of flavor and finesse as the world's most prominent chefs.

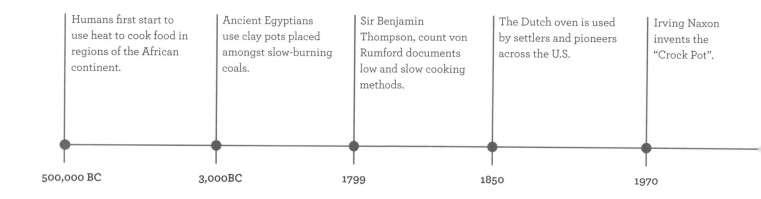

Humans first start to use heat to cook food in regions of the African continent.	Ancient Egyptians use clay pots placed amongst slow-burning coals.	Sir Benjamin Thompson, count von Rumford documents low and slow cooking methods.	The Dutch oven is used by settlers and pioneers across the U.S.	Irving Naxon invents the "Crock Pot".
500,000 BC	3,000BC	1799	1850	1970

SOUS VIDE INSIGHTS

Thomas Keller

Chef/Proprietor, Thomas Keller Restaurant Group

Sous vide is sometimes misunderstood. It is not about convenience. It is about precision and accuracy. What sous vide preparations have allowed us in the kitchen is consistency and a heightened sense of time management. You can cook a steak much faster conventionally than you can sous vide. But with conventional cooking, you must rely on your skills alone, and you still have a large margin of error. With sous vide technology and immersion cooking, you can identify a specific temperature for that steak and get it right every time. It will take you much longer to achieve, but it is worth the wait. This is where your skills are applied in sous vide preparations. You must not rush, just as in all types of preparations. Cooking is rewarding and should be fun. And part of that fun is the process.

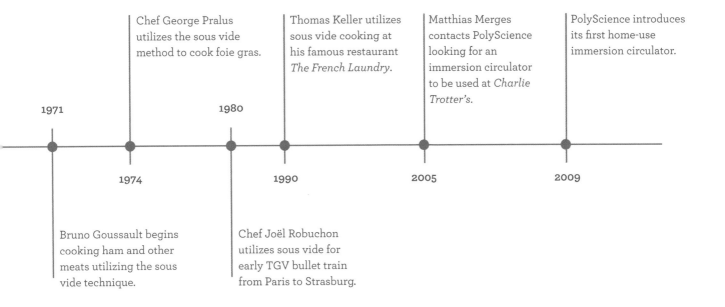

Chef George Pralus utilizes the sous vide method to cook foie gras.

Thomas Keller utilizes sous vide cooking at his famous restaurant *The French Laundry*.

Matthias Merges contacts PolyScience looking for an immersion circulator to be used at *Charlie Trotter's*.

PolyScience introduces its first home-use immersion circulator.

1971

1980

Bruno Goussault begins cooking ham and other meats utilizing the sous vide technique.

1974

Chef Joël Robuchon utilizes sous vide for early TGV bullet train from Paris to Strasburg.

1990

2005

2009

ESSENTIALS OF SOUS VIDE

TEMPERATURE

Sous vide cooking allows for cooking at a very specific temperature, often within one-tenth of one degree Fahrenheit. When cooking proteins, including beef, pork, fish and eggs, the ideal temperature is subjective, based primarily on the degree of doneness you hope to achieve. Consequently, temperature preferences may vary widely from chef to chef. Charts showing varying degrees of doneness for steak and salmon are shown below. When cooking foods such as vegetables, fruits and grains, however, setting more specific temperatures is the norm.

THICKNESS

The thickness of the food you are cooking determines how long it will take for its internal temperature to be as warm as the water around it. The best way to measure thickness is to use calipers, which can be purchased from most hardware or home-supply stores. Ingredients should always be measured at their thickest point, and it is often easier to measure in millimeters rather than inches to avoid fractions.

TIME

As with any cooking method, cooking time greatly impacts the textures and flavors of your food. When cooking sous vide, tough cuts, such as short ribs and beef brisket, benefit from longer cooking times. Conversely, relatively delicate foods such as fish, green vegetables and chicken breasts benefit from shorter cooking times once they've achieved their proper internal temperature. The charts below detail the differences in texture of beef and salmon as the cooking temperature varies. (Photos courtesy of CookingIssues.com)

A temperature probe takes any guesswork out of sous vide cooking.

Calipers are a great tool for measuring thickness to help predict cooking times.

| 122°F (50°C) | 124°F (51°C) | 127°F (53°C) | 131°F (55°C) | 135°F (57°C) | 138°F (59°C) | 140°F (60°C) | 142°F (61°C) | 145°F (63°C) | 149°F (65°C) | 153°F (67°C) | 156°F (69°C) | 160°F (71°C) | 162°F (72°C) |

raw → overcooked

| 118°F (48°C) | 122°F (50°C) | 126°F (52°C) | 129°F (54°C) | 133°F (56°C) | 136°F (58°C) | 140°F (60°C) | 144°F (62°C) |

raw → overcooked

FOOD SAFETY

Food safety is a complex subject that depends on a combination of factors, including temperature, time, pH level, the freshness of ingredients and even the age and health of the person consuming the food. Employing a set of simple yet practical food safety precautions is important when cooking sous vide. These steps only take a few moments, but go a long way toward making sure that your creations are as healthy as they are delicious.

- Use only the freshest ingredients for optimal flavor and results.

- Ensure hands, tools and work surfaces are clean.

- Make sure food is refrigerated at 38°F/3.3°C or below until ready to seal or cook.

- Check vacuum bags for a proper seal before cooking.

- Move products directly from refrigerated storage to preheated baths.

- Don't overload preheated baths with cold products because temperature recovery times may be significantly lengthened.

- When undertaking cook-and-chill recipes, use an ice bath to chill rapidly.

- If a bag becomes bloated, it is likely a sign of bacteria spoilage and should not be used.

- Additional safety information can be found on our website, PolyScienceCulinary.com.

BOILING POINT CURVE: THE EFFECT OF PRESSURE ON THE BOILING TEMPERATURE OF WATER

One of the most common sous vide mistakes is not cooling food before it is vacuum-sealed. As illustrated by the chart shown below, liquids, including those within food, can boil in chamber vacuum sealers if not properly chilled, thus making sealing difficult and producing tougher textures.

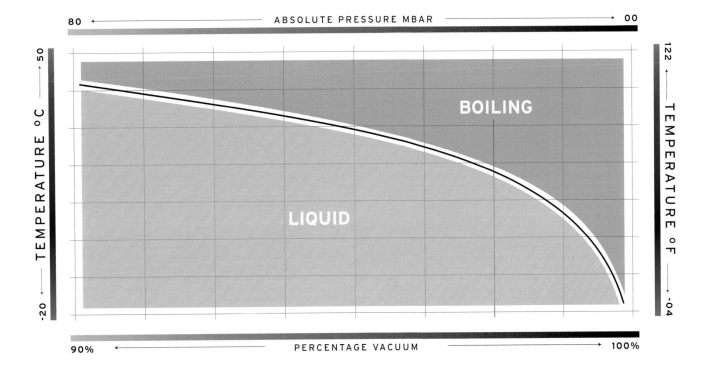

VARYING TIME & TEMPERATURE

Increasing the thickness of the food will increase cooking times exponentially. In fact, it is not uncommon for sous vide cooking times to quadruple when using slightly thicker ingredients than those outlined in this book. Increasing the bath temperature 1° or 2° Fahrenheit/1° Celsius will cut down cooking times dramatically, but you may see some "overcook" around the edges and notice a less supple texture.

So what should you do if you don't want to wait five hours for your pork chop? Raise your bath 1 to 2°F/1°C above your target core temp and probe the pork chop as it cooks so that the process can be stopped at the moment you reach the desired internal temperature of 145°F/62.7°C. To accomplish this precision, apply a ¾-inch piece of high density foam tape to the outside of the pouch and insert a hypodermic thermocouple type probe into the food. Make sure that the tip of the probe is at the very center of the thickest part of whatever you are cooking. The probe will indicate the exact temperature the cooking should stop.

COOKING VEGETABLES

Vegetable cookery is an area where sous vide really shines. Normally, vegetables cooked in boiling water or a hot oven will inevitably lose nutrients, color, flavor, and aromas, but when cooking them sous vide, all of these elements remain "sealed in the bag."

When cooking vegetables, pectin (the building block of plant life) breaks down around 185°F/85°C. Root vegetables like to be cooked at 181.4°F/83°C for three hours. If you are pressed for time or are cooking fruit, try cooking your vegetables and fruits at 183.2°F/84°C for about one hour. If you are looking for a more traditional texture for your vegetables and fruits, try cooking them at 185°F/85°C. At that temperature, cooking times will vary widely, as each unique fruit and vegetable will break down at different rates.

Cooking green vegetables sous vide was long regarded as a waste of time and effort. However, quickly cooking vegetables such as kale, green beans and asparagus at a high temperature — 194°F/90°C — followed by a thorough chilling in an ice bath works very well. These high temperatures, in conjunction with the reduction of air due to the vacuum packaging, prevent discoloration. The only drawback to blanching green vegetables cooked sous vide is that members of the cruciferous family — cabbage, broccoli, and bok choy — tend to yield undesirable aromas and take on drab appearances when left in the bag. Those foods should be removed from their vacuum pouch immediately after chilling in an ice bath.

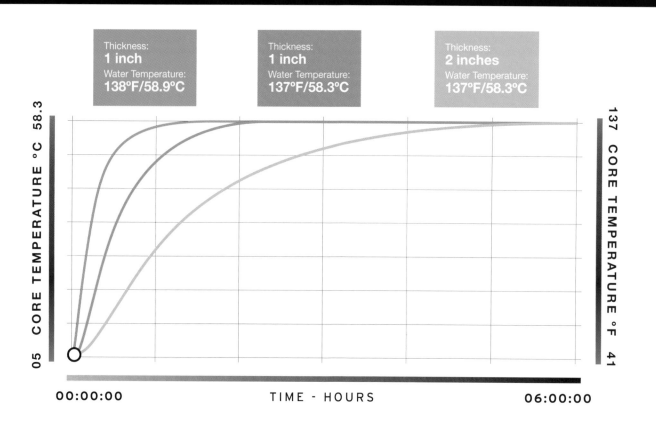

SOUS VIDE TOOLBOX™

In order to simplify the process, PolyScience® has developed its own Sous Vide Toolbox™ iPhone/iPad application, a practical tool for predicting core temperatures of the protein you're cooking. Users simply enter the type of protein they want to cook, along with its shape, size, starting temperature, water temperature and desired internal temperature, and the application automatically calculates the minimum cooking time.

We believe the software is a remarkable tool that can help everyone who cooks sous vide. Recently, we enlisted the help of the Hospitality Institute of Technology and Management's O. Peter Snyder Jr., Ph.D., a leading food safety expert to verify its accuracy and efficacy. Dr. Snyder concluded that the PolyScience® Sous Vide Toolbox™ application "is a professional aid (in) determining the time required for heating muscle foods in a controlled temperature water bath. Safety of a sous vide process is always verified by measuring the final core temperature of the food product with a temperature probe and meeting government food safety standards."

Dr. Snyder has also provided detailed insights to help our customers better understand and minimize sous vide-associated food safety risks. PolyScience® is committed to providing the tools and information needed to help both professional and home cooks safely navigate through every step of the sous vide process. Please see what Dr. Snyder has to say on pages 118 and 119.

The ▼ symbol appearing throughout the recipe section indicates PolyScience®'s Sous Vide Toolbox™ settings predicting the desired core temperature corresponding to specific bath temperatures.

Screenshots of the PolyScience® Sous Vide Toolbox™.

ONE DEGREE MAKES A DIFFERENCE

When cooking foods that do not require additional time for tenderness, raising the cooking temperature one degree above your desired core temperature will reduce the cooking time significantly without negatively affecting the end result. An example of this can be found in the recipe for Double-Cut Pork Chops, as shown in the "fast method" shortcut on page 85. The chart to the left demonstrates this variance in cooking time for a 1" thick steak with a target temperature of 137°F/58.3°C.

EQUIPMENT OVERVIEW

CHOOSING THE RIGHT VACUUM SEALER

Vacuum-sealed pouches were traditionally used for all sous vide cooking. The tight plastic film surrounding the food provides good heat transfer and keeps the pouch from floating to the surface of the bath. A well-sealed pouch guarantees your ingredients will cook evenly, surrounded by water on all sides.

Vacuum-sealed pouches remain popular. However, zip-top plastic kitchen bags are increasingly being used today as convenient alternatives. They can be easily secured to the sides of water baths with simple binder clips, thus remaining fully submerged for optimal cooking. Eggs, for example, can be cooked to perfection by placing them in a zip-top bag filled with water from the bath and secured to the vessel wall. In some instances, a glass jar filled with a cooking liquid may work best for your specific needs.

There are two types of vacuum-sealing devices, each is described in greater detail below.

Salmon filet vacuum-sealed with flat leaf parsley and olive oil.

CHAMBER VACUUM SEALERS

When using a chamber vacuum sealer, food-safe plastic pouches are placed completely within the machine. A vacuum pump sucks all of the air out from the chamber, ensuring that the plastic tightly conforms to the contents of each bag before it is sealed. Because air is sucked out of the bags from all directions, these machines ensure that braising liquids and marinades don't seep out from the bag or interfere with the sealing process. The speed of chamber vacuum sealers makes them advantageous for restaurants and high-volume cooking environments.

PolyScience® 300 Series Chamber Vacuum Sealer

EXTERNAL VACUUM SEALERS

An external vacuum sealer is a vacuum pump device that is clamped to the outside of a bag. It sucks out as much air as possible from one direction. External vacuum sealers are generally lightweight, small and less expensive than chamber vacuum sealers, but more care must be taken to avoid liquids being drawn out during the sealing process. The sealing process also tends to be slower than those used in chamber sealers.

Regardless of which type of vacuum-sealing method you choose, it is important to understand the effects of the vacuum process.

PolyScience® 200 Series External Vacuum Sealer

*PolyScience® Sous Vide DISCOVERY Immersion Circulator —
Typical Home Setup*

*PolyScience® Sous Vide Professional™ CHEF Series
Immersion Circulator — Typical Professional Setup*

EQUIPMENT SET-UP

The most common type of sous vide bath is composed of three main components: an immersion circulator, a vessel to hold the water, and the water itself. In the example to the left, the PolyScience® Sous Vide Discovery Immersion Circulator unit is shown attached to a standard stockpot, which can be found in most home kitchens. Below, you can see the PolyScience® Sous Vide Professional™ CHEF Series Immersion Circulator attached to a polycarbonate tank that can be purchased at a restaurant supply store in your local area. From a practical standpoint there is a clear benefit of being able to see your food as it cooks, but either type of bath setup will provide the same results.

SIZE OF BATH & WATER VOLUME

There are two key elements to consider when setting up your water bath. What is the size of your bath? And how much water are you using? Larger amounts of water will take longer to heat, but will be more effective at maintaining their temperature when chilled sous vide pouches are added to the bath. Smaller baths will heat faster but will be susceptible to a significant lag time for the bath to regain its target temperature once chilled sous vide pouches of food are added. The key is to find a bath that is just the right size. A general rule of thumb is that the minimum bath would be 8 quarts (2 gallons / 7.6 Liters), and the largest that should be used with a single immersion circulator would be 32 quarts (8 gallons / 30 Liters).

Maintaining good water circulation is integral to the sous vide cooking process, so make sure to avoid placing too many pouches into any one sous vide water bath. A 50 percent product-to-water ratio is the generally accepted upper limit.

TEMPERATURE FLUCTUATION AND CIRCULATION

We can't overemphasize how critical good water circulation is to the sous vide cooking process. Consequently, we recommend using equipment with strong circulation capabilities. You should also avoid placing too many pouches into any one sous vide water bath. A 50 percent product-to-water ratio is the generally accepted upper limit.

ANATOMY OF A CIRCULATOR

Now that we've covered the basics behind sous vide cooking, let's take an even closer look at the equipment, itself.

Simply clamping an immersion circulator — the device that generates heat for the sous vide cooking process — to a tank or vessel can transform a water bath into a precisely controlled, integrated cooking system.

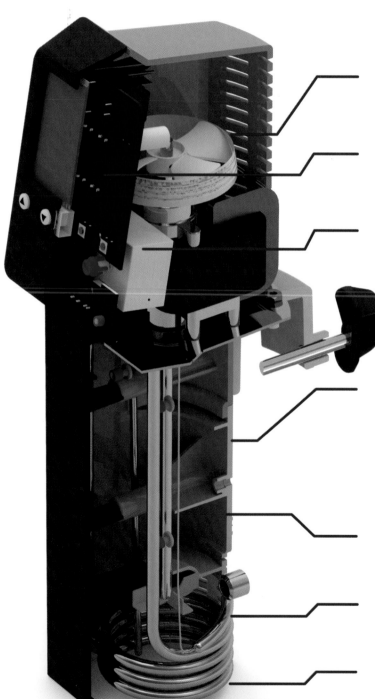

OVERVIEW
The best circulators consist of a pump, heater, a redundant safety thermostat and control electronics all housed within an intelligently designed framework.

TEMPERATURE FLUCTUATION & CIRCULATION
The ideal circulators are equipped with a pump. By circulating the water, the pump creates a uniform temperature throughout the bath, thus allowing you to cook food evenly.

VARIABLE POWER PERFORMANCE
A user-friendly Proportional-Integral-Derivative (PID) control system will facilitate rapid heat production and precise control.

FAIL-SAFE FEATURE
The safety system protects you and the circulator from overheating; the system automatically shuts down if set parameters are exceeded.

INTELLIGENT DESIGN
The design of circulators requires that a wide array of attributes be considered to ensure the devices are rugged yet user-friendly. For many professional and home users, size and weight are key criteria by which circulators are initially judged, but other aspects should not be overlooked. Temperatures should be easy to set and view throughout the cooking process.

EASY TO CLEAN
Easy access to the pump and heater for cleaning food and removing mineral deposits is essential.

HEATER PERFORMANCE & COOKING CAPACITY
The heater is activated by a control system to bring the bath to a desired temperature.

SAFETY FEATURES
Circulators should not have any sharp protrusions that could damage bags, and the heater within each unit should be properly isolated to prevent it from melting any pouches that it might touch.

This is a new piece of equipment for me, and I am looking forward to using it and discovering another way to cook my old favorites.

Jacques Pepin -
Renowned chef, restaurateur and author

A CONTRIBUTION FROM BRUNO GOUSSAULT

Sous vide pioneer Bruno Goussault leading a culinary seminar at Kendall College in Chicago.

It is natural to ask why anyone would want to cook sous vide. The simple answer would be to cook at precise temperatures. And in order to cook at very precise temperatures, one needs to cook in water or vapor. To cook in water, one needs to protect products against the "washing away" of flavors. In modern sous vide cooking, that protection often takes the form of polyethylene or polyamide plastic pouches into which the ingredients are packaged.

To properly cook meat, fish or vegetables with that type of plastic "skin," one needs to use a vacuum sealer. That device must have the capability to pump enough air out of the pouch to obtain a good transfer of heat between the food and the water while not distorting the product's shape.

That is sous vide cooking at its most basic. More broadly, sous vide cooking is about cooking technology, and to cook, one wants to achieve two objectives:

1. Develop the sensory quality of food
  • Create or maintain attractive colors
  • Obtain pleasing textures and tenderness
  • Extract, enhance and fix flavors
  • Capture juiciness and moisture

2. Create safe products with adequate shelf lives
  • Destroy all vegetative forms of pathogenic bacteria
  • Block the germination of pathogenic bacteria spores
  • Develop a positive equilibrium between preservatives and spoilage bacteria

Let's take a closer look. The first objective of any cooking is to develop sensory advantages and obtain a "good" product. To best accomplish this, one needs to work at precise temperatures, and to do that, one needs to measure core temperatures. This precise temperature management permits one to correctly extract flavors and aromas; however, you also need to lock them in.

Bruno Goussault set out to quantify and better understand broader applications of the sous vide cooking method. He has likely had more influence over the understanding and adaptation of sous vide cooking than anyone else. In fact, he has trained 43 three-starred Michelin chefs to date! He remains active in the field as the Chief Scientist at both CREA, The Culinary Research and Education Academy, and Cuisine Solutions, Inc.,

Whenever one "cooks and serves," you often lose the most important results of the cooking technique. For example when a sous vide pouch is opened after cooking, the flavors often evaporate and are lost if they aren't fixed. As a result, a two-step post-cooking chilling process has been devised.

Traditionally, at the end of cooking, if one wants to preserve products, then one has to chill them to 50°F/10°C in less than one hour and maintain them at about 32°-37°F/0°-3° C to block germination of spores of pathogenic bacteria until one is ready to re-therm them. However, if one wants to better fix flavors in the core of meat and fish and keep the exudate fluid, one should first maintain the product after cooking for 10 minutes at room temperature until the core temperature arrives at its maximum and begins to decrease. Then as a second step, the product should be held for 10 minutes in 64°F/18°C circulating water to keep any gelatin coming from the hydrolysis of connective tissues and any fat melted in the cooking liquefied.

This part of the sous vide process is important in order to fix flavor in the core of meat and fish because the water-holding capacity of muscle remains active below 154°F/68°C. Meat and fish are able to absorb a part of the very good exudate only if it stays liquid. This is exactly the same process chefs use at the end of classical cooking, like roasting beef, when they rest products for 15 minutes at kitchen ambient temperature to fix exudates. The products then need to be stored for two hours in an iced water bath or in blast chillers to prepare it for the refrigerator and temperatures around 32°F/0°C.

Moving beyond meat and fish, let's look at how we can define precise temperatures for vegetables and why we recommend cooking them at 181°F/83°C for three to four hours. Here's the challenge: Most people like to eat vegetables "al dente," and in order to achieve this result, chefs stop the cooking in boiling water or in vapor after two minutes when the starch is still raw and indigestible. To figure out an answer, we need to look at vegetables in more detail.

> Vegetables have four basic components: cellulose, protopectin, starch or derivated sugars and water. All have different temperature limits.
>
> The temperature limit to hydrolyze cellulose is above 248°F/120°C, which we never reach with sous vide cooking, but is needed to insure the intestinal transit.
>
> Pectin is the "stick" for adherence between cells and is responsible for the crispiness of raw vegetables. The temperature limit to hydrolyze pectin is 185°F/85°C.
>
> Starch needs to be hydrolyzed to be digestible, and the temperature limit is 172°F/78°C.

Fortunately, there is a temperature to cook vegetables where starches are hydrolyzed and digestible and where the pectin is still raw: below 185°F/85°C. Although we recommend 178-181°F/81-83°C, you must remember that in this temperature range the cooking time is multiplied by ten in order to hydrolyze starch. Also don't forget to add oil or butter to fix the aromas of the vegetables because the natural element for this fixation is hydrolyzed pectin and when you cook at 181°F/83°C you respect protopectin and don't produce hydrolyzed pectin. In vegetables there is no reabsorption of exudate. Instead one just needs to chill products and fix the flavor of oils and butter. Also, be careful as starch does not support ice water.

Let's now look at the second objective of cooking: obtaining safe products and products with long shelf lives. These two points depend on management of bacteria. In 1993, CREA, the Culinary Research & Education Academy, first published results of studies on the behavior of vegetative forms of pathogenic bacteria in sous vide cooking at precise temperatures. We continue to follow this behavior today and find that vegetative forms of bacteria begin to be destroyed at 125°F/52°C. Total destruction occurs, even in the cores of meat and fish, at 132°F/56°C. However the new "step-by-step" process introduces better safety security.

The most important contamination to consider is on the surface of the products. Therefore, the first step is to place it in a water bath set at 181°F/83°C which destroys more than 10 log of all vegetative forms of mesophilic bacteria in three minutes. Many chefs try to decrease the ambient temperature of cooking below

125°F/52°C and stop the core temperature cooking around 107°F/42°C especially for fish because they like the resulting taste and texture, but care must be taken. At these temperatures the vegetative forms of bacteria are never destroyed. Instead, at those temperatures of incubation, you increase the level of pathogenic bacteria and increase the hazard of food poisoning. "Warm Sushi and Sashimi" (Sushi and Sashimi Chaud) is what one produces at those temperatures.

Do I have the same view on food and cooking as you? Perhaps as a result of not being able to see the world around me as everybody else does, I have a different perception of the elements which compose it. Yes, I am totally blind to color, and when I look at something that has a different color, and then all the people around you talk about this object and its color, I try to understand what the differences are.

When I look at a stoplight in the street, everybody stops when the light is red and passes when the light is green. If one is color blind, one needs to look at the position of the light. If the light is on top, one will stop. If the light is on the bottom, one will pass. And one passes through the stoplight after a storm and the stoplight has been flipped upside down, there is a possibility that one would receive a traffic violation ticket if a policeman were to see this event.

It's the same concept in my expertise. Food products may have many colors during their lifespan, and people discuss the beautiful colors of green apples or the bad colors of non-matured apples or cooked vegetables which contain chlorophylls. In meat, I can identify the differences between a beautifully aged piece of red beef and one that has gone green from improper preservation because the texture of the meat of these two colors is not the same; actually, it is extremely different. I understand that difference when I want to explain what happens when - and why- meat colors change during maturation and alteration. Usually, people who see color do not see it because their views are absorbed only by color. When one is color blind, he/she has a drastically different view of the objects in one's life.

The color of food makes a difference.

STEP BY STEP SOUS VIDE SUCCESS

Sous vide cooking can be simple and straightforward if you invest the necessary time and energy. The following chart represents the entire sous vide cooking process. The checks (✓) represent suggested steps and the crosses (✗) represent actions you should avoid.

FOR INSTRUCTIONAL VIDEOS, VISIT POLYSCIENCECULINARY.COM

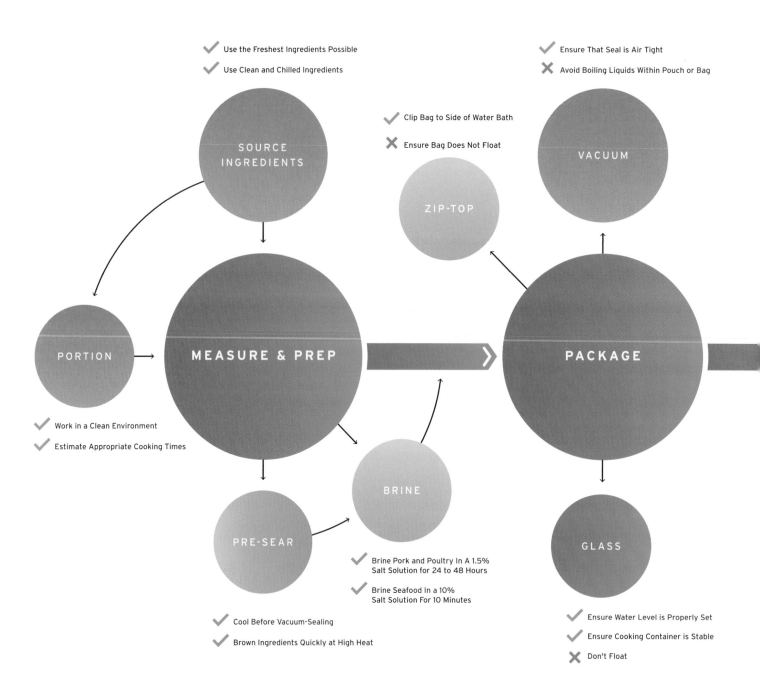

✓ Use the Freshest Ingredients Possible
✓ Use Clean and Chilled Ingredients

✓ Clip Bag to Side of Water Bath
✗ Ensure Bag Does Not Float

✓ Ensure That Seal is Air Tight
✗ Avoid Boiling Liquids Within Pouch or Bag

SOURCE INGREDIENTS

ZIP-TOP

VACUUM

PORTION

MEASURE & PREP

PACKAGE

✓ Work in a Clean Environment
✓ Estimate Appropriate Cooking Times

BRINE

PRE-SEAR

✓ Brine Pork and Poultry In A 1.5% Salt Solution for 24 to 48 Hours
✓ Brine Seafood In a 10% Salt Solution For 10 Minutes

GLASS

✓ Cool Before Vacuum-Sealing
✓ Brown Ingredients Quickly at High Heat

✓ Ensure Water Level is Properly Set
✓ Ensure Cooking Container is Stable
✗ Don't Float

Maintain Temperature of Tough Meat to Tenderize

Do Not Hold Temperature of Tender Meat

Discard All Bloated Bags

HOLD

PAN-SEAR

TORCH

Measure Thickest Section of Ingredient

Use Sous Vide Toolbox™ Application

Check Internal Temperature with Probe

COOK

FINISH

OPEN & SERVE

RE-THERM

Re-heat Ingredients to 2ºF/1ºC
Below Desired Internal Temperature

CRYO-FRY

CHILL

BROIL

Cool to at Least 38ºF/3ºC

Place in Ice Bath Before Refrigerating

Do Not Refrigerate Immediately Without Cooling in an Ice Bath First

RECIPES

The recipes on the following pages, which are organized according to different mealtimes, have been selected to serve as a springboard for your sous vide journey. Several recipes — indicated by a ▼ — provide a list of cooking parameters that correspond to the PolyScience® Sous Vide Toolbox™ app, the online tool that takes the guesswork out of sous vide cooking.

Solid fundamental skills are the building blocks of any professional chef's or home cook's repertoire. Therefore, these recipes were written not only to be delicious but also to teach you the underlying principles at work during the sous vide cooking process.

The required quantities of the ingredients needed for the upcoming recipes are listed in both volume and weight. We prefer to measure ingredients by weight (grams) rather than by volume. Tablespoons, teaspoons, cups, and other traditional measurements can lead to complex fractions when scaling a recipe up or down. Depending on the manufacturer of the volume-measuring tool that you are using, volumes may vary, creating inconsistencies. Remember that 500 grams will always weigh 500 grams. Therefore, for best results, follow the recipes using weight, noting that most low-cost gram scales that are capable of sustaining up to 10 pounds of weight either perform poorly or not at all below 10 grams (and they are certainly inaccurate when weighing ingredients under 1 gram). For this reason, it is best to buy a jeweler's scale for measuring very light ingredients and small amounts.

For best results, thinner liquids such as the peach gin, bitters and glögg were strained through a #200 geological sieve. In the restaurant world, this device is called a tamis. Thick sauces, soups and purees can be strained through a chinois. A chinois, or "China cap," is a fine-mesh conical sieve used to strain sauces.

When buying a thermometer, if possible, look for one that accepts an RTD-type probe for best accuracy. Thermocouple-based thermometers are easy to find and use, but it should be noted that you will likely see variance in temperature compared to your immersion circulator. That difference is based on the inherent inaccuracy in the thermocouple compared to the probe in your immersion circulator. It will also help if your thermometer offers data-logging capabilities, a temperature-hold feature and the ability to set high and low temperature limits. When writing recipes that require an oven, temperatures have been rounded to the nearest whole degree.

One final tip: Although sous vide cooking is a very exact cooking method, try to take the time to recognize the aromas, sounds and visual cues of a well-cooked meal. Cooking is largely a sensory experience. Becoming more in tune with your cooking environment will make you a faster, cleaner and smarter cook. Take notes and photographs of the things that you cook. It is very easy to forget small details while preparing meals for a busy night's service or a friendly get-together. It is these small details that separate great cooks from mediocre ones, whether at home or in a restaurant.

Most importantly, I hope you have fun on your sous vide journey.

Note: Recipes reference Imperial / U.S. cup, tablespoon, and teaspoon

BREAKFAST

Sous vide allows chefs to control temperatures. That's what it's all about, the ability to control your heat to one one-hundredth of a degree. With sous vide you are able to take a product, like an artichoke or a piece of lamb, and cook it to your exact preference. Your lamb can be rare or medium rare; you can cook your artichokes so they have a bit of an al dente bite or are a little softer in a French style. You're able to cook the pieces of vegetable to that degree every single time and maintain that temperature every single time. If you have the tendency to overcook or undercook your food, sous vide gives you a really great method of control. It breaks down some of the sinews and fibers so it becomes more tender. With sous vide, your cooking takes on a different dimension.

Matthias Merges
Former Executive Chef of Charlie Trotter's, Chef & Owner of Yusho Restaurant

HOLLANDAISE SAUCE

It's hard to imagine some dishes, especially those served for brunch, without hollandaise, the classic French egg sauce. When preparing hollandaise, there are all sorts of things that can go wrong, but one of the most common mistakes involves scrambling the yolks while whisking them, which can occur even if you're skilled in using a double boiler. Not only is it easy to overcook the yolks, you also run the risk of getting burned. And if you allow your hollandaise to get too hot or too cold, the emulsion will break, and the sauce will look curdled and greasy. Sous vide cooking eliminates all of these potential pitfalls.

Parameters:

Cook Time: 30 minutes
Temperature: 158°F / 70°C
Serves: 6

Ingredients:

1 tablespoon / 13 grams white wine

2 tablespoons + 2 teaspoons / 30 grams champagne vinegar

1 each / 25 grams shallot, thinly sliced

1 each thyme sprig

2-1/2 tablespoons / 20 grams lemon juice

5-6 each / 85 grams egg yolks

1/4 cup / 60 grams water

1 stick + 2 tablespoons / 150 grams unsalted butter

3/4 teaspoon / 3 grams salt

Special Equipment:

1-liter whipping siphon, 2 nitrous oxide charges (shown below)

Method:

1. Preheat a water bath to 158°F / 70°C.

2. In a small pot, combine the wine, vinegar, shallot and thyme. Reduce the mixture by half and strain out the solids. Chill and reserve 2-1/2 tablespoons / 20 grams of the reduction.

3. Place the chilled reduction, egg yolks, lemon juice, water, butter and salt in a vacuum pouch and vacuum-seal.

4. Place the vacuum pouch into the water bath and cook sous vide for 30 minutes.

5. Remove the egg yolk mixture from the water bath and pour the contents of the pouch into a 1-liter whipping siphon. Charge the siphon with 2 nitrous oxide charges, shaking the canister vigorously between adding each charge. Using a PolyScience® whipping siphon holder, clip the canister to a water bath heated to 149°F / 65°C to hold the hollandaise warm.

6. Distribute as foam and immediately serve.

Cooking egg yolks separately from other ingredients to a perfect temperature increases their emulsifying power. With that in mind, try cooking the egg yolks for your mayonnaise and other egg-based sauces before blending in your fat of choice. This step will help them "come together." It will also pasteurize the yolks, eliminating any concerns you may have about eating raw eggs.

EGGS BENEDICT

Preparing a perfectly poached egg is a fine art. Everyone has their own tricks and tips, but poaching eggs sous vide is by far the easiest way to get it just right. Learn this technique and rubbery whites and overly runny yolks will become a distant memory. Eggs poached sous vide are incredibly versatile, helping you transform simple salads, pastas and a host of mundane breakfast offerings into silkier and more nuanced creations.

Ingredients:

eggs
hollandaise as needed
canadian bacon

Input data for Sous Vide Toolbox™

Units:	in / mm °F / °C
Food Selection:	Eggs-Low Slow Method
Shape:	Diameter
Thickness:	1 3/4 in / 44 mm
Cooking Method:	Time to Temperature
Desired Core Temperature:	147.2°F / 64°C
Initial Temperature:	41°F / 5°C
Water Temperature:	147.2°F / 64°C
Tenderness Time:	Off
Ice Bath:	Off
Cook Time:	51 minutes

Method:

1. Preheat your water bath to the desired temperature based on the texture you want to achieve.

2. Carefully place the eggs into a vacuum pouch or zip-top bag.

3. Once the water bath has reached the desired temperature, carefully ladle bath water into the bag containing the eggs to keep them from moving around the bath. Once all of the eggs are fully submerged, lower the bag into the water bath and clip it to the side of the container.

4. Cook the egg for the amount of time outlined in our Input Data for Sous Vide Toolbox™ (to the left, below) or reference the chart on page 19. The temperature of an egg will usually equalize with the bath temperature in 50 to 60 minutes.

5. Gently crack the egg open onto a paper towel to capture any excess liquid and egg white. Carefully roll the egg into its serving position.

In order to prepare your eggs in advance, plunge them into a heavily iced bath immediately after cooking. The eggs may be rewarmed to 135°F / 57.2°C in about 25 minutes using a bath set to 140°F / 60°C. Eggs can be held at 140°F / 60°C for approximately 120 minutes without fear of overcooking. The proteins will begin to denature after 120 minutes, resulting in unpleasant textures, so avoid cooking them too long.

If you are cooking the eggs to various temperatures, you can keep track of them by writing directly on their shells with food-safe marking pens to record warming times, temperatures and other cooking information.

Everyone has different preferences when it comes to the tastes and textures of their food. For those who desire firmer whites, consider placing the egg into simmering water for 30-45 seconds either before or immediately after they warm up in the sous vide bath. Alternatively, some people prefer cooking eggs at higher temperatures for shorter periods of time, while others like to rewarm an egg by cracking it open and releasing it into barely simmering water to firm up the whites. Sous vide cooking is versatile enough to accommodate these different various tastes.

FRENCH TOAST

PolyScience® chef David Pietranczyk claims he won over his girlfriend with this recipe. It produces toast with an incredible custard-like crème brûlée texture, and when you crisp the outside, the results will make you and your guests positively swoon with delight. You can prepare this one-of-a-kind take on French toast for breakfast, brunch, lunch or even dessert. Topped with whipped cream, our bourbon-infused peaches (below) or bacon-shallot jam (page 69), it's as versatile as it is delicious.

Parameters:

Cook Time: 1 hour, 30 minutes
Temperature: 147.2°F / 64°C
Thickness: 1 1/4 inch / 32 mm
Yield: 6 slices

Ingredients:

1 cup / 205 grams heavy whipping cream

1 cup / 214 grams 2% milk

7 tablespoons / 57 grams sugar

2 teaspoons / 10 grams vanilla extract

4 each / 197 grams whole eggs

1/4 teaspoon / 1 gram kosher salt to taste

6 each (1 1/4 inch / 31.75 mm) thick slices challah bread

1/2 tablespoon / 7.5 grams unsalted butter

bourbon-infused peaches as desired

whipped cream as desired

When filling vacuum bags, fold the opening of the vacuum pouch backwards over itself to make sure it remains dry and seals properly.

Method:

1. Preheat a water bath to 147.2°F / 64°C.

2. Combine the milk, cream, vanilla and half of the sugar in a small pot over medium heat. Meanwhile, whisk the eggs and the remainder of the sugar in a bowl large enough to accommodate the dairy mixture as well, whisking until the eggs and sugar are light in color.

3. When the milk mixture comes to a boil, take the pot off the heat and very slowly begin to drizzle it into the eggs, whisking constantly. Cool the egg-dairy mixture completely.

4. Cut six slices from a loaf of challah bread that are 1 1/4 inch / 32 mm thick. Dredge the slices in the chilled custard until well absorbed.

5. Fold the opening of the vacuum pouch over itself. Place the dredged pieces of bread in the bag, making sure that the bread remains in a single layer and isn't overcrowded.

6. Gently vacuum the pouch so that the bread retains most of its shape. The bags will want to float, but it is crucial that they stay submerged during the cooking process, so make sure to weigh the bags down. Place the vacuum pouches into the water bath with the weight of your choice directly on top and cook for 1 hour and 30 minutes.

7. Carefully remove the bag from the heated bath and place it in a heavily iced bath to chill completely.

8. To finish the French toast, remove bread from the vacuum pouch and melt the butter in a non-stick pan over medium heat. Season the French toast lightly with salt and place it in the pan. Cover the pan with a lid and cook until the toast begins to brown. Flip the toast and repeat on the other side. (Covering the toast will help it warm while it is searing.) Serve immediately.

BOURBON-INFUSED PEACHES

When using the sous vide method, you don't need expansive amounts of liquid in order to perform a perfect poach. A little liquid goes a long way. We'll let the results of this recipe speak for themselves.

Parameters:

Cook Time: 45 minutes
Temperature: 181.4°F / 83°C
Thickness: 1 1/4 inch / 32 mm
Serves: 4

Ingredients:

4 each / 1,072 grams peaches, peeled, pitted, cut in half

1/2 cup / 120 grams water

1 cup / 230 grams brown sugar

1 each star anise

2 each allspice berries

1/8 cup / 26 grams bourbon

Method:

1. Preheat a water bath to 181.4°F / 83°C.

2. Combine the brown sugar, spices and water in a small saucepan and bring to a boil. Remove the syrup from the heat and strain out the spices. Cool completely and add the bourbon.

3. Place the peach halves and syrup in a vacuum pouch and vacuum-seal, taking care to keep the peaches in one single layer.

4. Place the vacuum pouch in the bath and cook for 45 minutes.

5. Once the peaches have been cooked, they may be sliced and served warm, or chilled and served cold.

YOGURT

Your sous vide system is ideal for making yogurt, eliminating the need to buy a yogurt machine or pay inflated prices at the grocery store. Simply heat milk gently on the stove top and use your sous vide bath as a precise temperature-controlled yogurt maker. We suggest adding a blueberry compote and granola (see page 45) or creating your own individual toppings.

Parameters:

Cook Time: 8 hours
Temperature: 106°F / 41.1°C
Yield: 8 cups

Ingredients:

8 cups / 1957 grams whole milk
1/2 cups / 140 grams live active culture yogurt, room temperature

Special Equipment:

1-liter whipping siphon, 2 nitrous oxide charges

You can use store-bought yogurt with active cultures as a starter. Just place the container of the purchased yogurt on the lid of the bath to warm it as you heat the milk on the stove top. Both will be ready to combine at the same time. It should reach room temperature until the milk cools to 110°F / 43.4°C.

Method:

1. Preheat a water bath to 106°F / 41.1°C.

2. Bring the milk to 185°F / 85°C in a pot on the stove, stirring gently to avoid scorching the bottom.

3. Once the milk reaches 185°F / 85°C, remove it from the heat.

4. Cool the milk to 110°F / 43.4°C. Whisk the yogurt into a small portion of the milk and add it back to the pot. Take care not to let the temperature drop below 90°F / 32.2°C or you will need to start over.

5. Divide the mixture evenly amongst three 1-quart mason jars. Screw the lids on securely.

6. Place the jars in the water bath, making sure that the water level is even with the level of the liquid in the jars. If the levels are uneven, the jars will float. Based on the vessel you choose, you may need to elevate the jars slightly by placing a support underneath them.

7. Cover the water bath and allow the yogurt to hold at 106°F / 41.1°C for 8 hours.

8. Remove the yogurt jars from the water bath and place them in the refrigerator to chill thoroughly. For a Greek-style yogurt, you may hang the yogurt in cheesecloth to strain out the whey. Hanging times will vary based on your desired texture.

BLUEBERRY COMPOTE

Blueberry compote is easy to make, adding a perfectly balanced lilt of sugar and acidity to a host of dishes. Use it on yogurt, ice cream, waffles, pancakes and much more. The same recipe can be used to create different kinds of compotes using different kinds of berries, so go ahead and experiment.

Parameters:

Cook Time: 20 minutes
Temperature: 185°F / 85°C
Yield: 1 cup

Ingredients:

4 cups / 523 grams blueberries
1/3 cup / 67 grams sugar
1 each / 4 grams cinnamon stick
2 inch piece / 33 grams ginger, peeled, sliced

Method:

1. Place your immersion circulator on your desired cooking vessel and preheat the water bath to 185°F / 85°C.

2. Combine all of the ingredients in a vacuum pouch and vacuum-seal it.

3. Place the vacuum pouch in the preheated water bath and cook it for 20 minutes.

4. Place the vacuum pouch in a heavily iced bath and chill completely.

5. Strain the liquid from the compote and reserve the solids. Discard the cinnamon stick and ginger.

GRANOLA

Besides being an ideal topping for yogurt, granola can be wonderful in muffins, serve as a simple breakfast when combined with milk or simply used as a crumble topping for custards and other desserts. Although this isn't a recipe that employs sous vide, we've included it because granola is such a versatile complement to so many foods. We suggest you use this recipe as a starting point and then try other seed, nut and dried-fruit combinations.

Parameters:

Cook Time: 1 hour
Yield: 3 quarts

Ingredients:

3 cups / 317 grams rolled oats
1/2 cup / 95 grams almonds
1/2 cup / 62 grams unsweetened coconut flakes
1/2 cup / 75 grams sunflower seed kernels
1/2 cup / 88 grams dried cherries
1/2 cup / 94 grams dried pineapple
1/2 cup / 100 grams vegetable oil
1/2 cup / 160 grams honey
1/4 cup / 41 grams chia seed

Method:

1. Preheat an oven to 250°F / 120°C.

2. Combine all of the ingredients in a bowl and mix well to evenly coat all of the ingredients in the honey and oil.

3. Line a sheet tray with aluminum foil and spray it lightly with nonstick cooking spray.

4. Spread the mixture in a thin, even layer on the sheet tray.

5. Place the sheet tray in the oven and bake for 1 hour, stirring the mixture halfway through baking.

6. Allow the granola to cool before placing it in an air-tight canister for storage.

LUNCH

Sous vide is probably the most convenient, efficient and least labor-intensive way that a home cook can accomplish restaurant cookery. We can draw parallels to what happened in the past. You can say, "My grandmother used a crock pot in the 1960s. And further down the road, in the late 1970s and 1980s, there was the convenience of frozen dinners that you would throw in the microwave. Sous vide, in terms of convenience, is similar if not better than those items because it allows you to customize the healthier, more exacting, meals that we all want today.

Grant Achatz
Chef & Owner of Alinea, Next, and The Aviary

SMOKED RANCH DRESSING

We've received rave reviews for this dressing recipe. While not prepared using the sous vide method, this recipe does use The Smoking Gun®, a unique handheld cold-smoking device. The smoky ranch dressing brightens a wide array of foods that can be cooked sous vide, including our recipe for mashed Yukon Gold potatoes (see page 66). The results are extraordinary, a creamy mashed potato puree brimming with the perfect balance of smoke, garlic and spice.

Parameters:
Cook Time: 15 minutes
Yield: 2 cups

Ingredients:
1 cup / 235 grams buttermilk
1/2 cup / 106 grams mayonnaise
4 tablespoons / 60 grams sour cream
1/4 cup / 11 grams parsley, chopped
1/4 cup / 11 grams cilantro, chopped
1 tablespoon / 3 grams chive, thinly sliced
2 each / 11 grams garlic cloves, minced
1/4 teaspoon / 1 gram piment d'espelette
1/2 teaspoon / 1 gram onion powder
1/4 teaspoon / 1 gram black pepper, cracked
1 tablespoon / 13 grams lemon juice

Method:

1. Whisk all the ingredients together in a container with a tight-fitting lid.

2. Insert the latex tube of The Smoking Gun® into the container and fill it with a dense smoke. Cover the container.

3. Allow the ranch to smoke for 5 minutes.

4. Remove the lid and whisk the dressing. Repeat the smoking step.

5. Remove the dressing and serve.

Special Equipment:
The Smoking Gun®, a handheld cold-smoking device
PolyScience® Classic Smokehouse hickory wood chips
Find more information at PolyScienceCulinary.com.

BUFFALO CHICKEN WINGS

This is a quick and easy way to make a classic party-food snack. Simply sous vide the wings ahead of time and chill them in their sealed pouches until you're ready to serve. They'll be fully cooked, tender and ready for a quick dip in the fryer.

Ingredients:

8 each / 256 grams chicken wing flats
8 each / 309 grams chicken wing drumettes
4 tablespoons / 44 grams olive oil
cornstarch as needed
buffalo wing sauce as needed

Input data for Sous Vide Toolbox™

Units:	in / mm °F / °C
Protein:	Poultry
Shape:	Whole Thigh/Leg
Thickness:	3/4 inch / 19 mm
Cooking Method:	Cook and Pasteurize to Core
Desired Core Temperature:	149°F / 65°C
Initial Temperature:	41°F / 5°C
Water Temperature:	149°F / 65°C
Ice Bath Temperature:	33.8°F / 1°C
Final Food Temperature:	41°F / 5°C
Serves:	3

Calculated Time:

Cook Time:	1 hour, 27 minutes
Cooling Time:	29 minutes
Total Time:	1 hour, 56 minutes

Method:

1. Preheat a water bath to 149°F / 65°C.

2. Combine the chicken wing flats with 2 tablespoons / 22 grams of the olive oil and vacuum-seal it. Repeat the procedure with the drumettes.

3. Place the vacuum pouches into the preheated water bath and cook them for 1 hour and 27 minutes.

4. When the wings have finished cooking, place the pouches in a heavily iced bath and allow them to chill thoroughly.

5. Preheat a fryer to 375°F / 190.5°C.

6. Remove the wings from the vacuum pouch and dry them completely with paper towels.

7. Toss the wings in cornstarch to coat them evenly. Shake off the excess cornstarch.

8. Fry the chicken pieces for 5 minutes and allow them to drain on a paper towel.

9. Toss the chicken pieces with the buffalo sauce. Serve.

MAC & CHEESE

Traditionally, mac & cheese is made with a heavy roux and lots of cheese. Here we take a different approach based on a hint from our friends at Modernist Cuisine and replace the béchamel with sodium citrate. Don't be put off by the formal name. Sodium citrate can be readily found in many retailers and for purchase on the internet. Rest assured, any extra effort needed to hunt down sodium citrate is well worth the effort because when combined with cheese, it results in an amazingly smooth and supple sauce like nothing you've ever tasted before.

Parameters:
Cook Time: 15 minutes
Temperature: 167°F / 75°C
Serves: 5

Ingredients:
1 cup / 150 grams smoked gouda, cubed
1 cup / 150 grams aged sharp cheddar, cubed
1 1/4 cup / 300 grams whole milk
2 teaspoons / 12 grams sodium citrate
1 pound / 453 grams pasta, cooked
garlic bread crumbs as needed

Method:

1. Preheat a water bath to 167°F / 75°C.

2. Combine the smoked gouda, sharp cheddar, milk, and sodium citrate in a vacuum pouch and vacuum-seal it.

3. Place the vacuum pouch in the preheated water bath and cook for 15 minutes.

4. Remove the pouch from the water bath and empty the contents into a blender. Blend until smooth.

5. Gently fold the cheese sauce into the cooked pasta and top it with garlic bread crumbs.

GARLIC BREAD CRUMBS

Garlic bread crumbs are an incredibly versatile accoutrement to have in your kitchen. They can add wonderful texture, flavor, visual appeal and aroma to a number of other recipes. So go ahead and sprinkle some on your next bowl of mac & cheese and consider using them as a garnish to your other favorite dishes and meals.

Parameters:
Cook Time: 20 minutes
Yield: 1 cup

Ingredients:
1 cup / 173 grams whole garlic cloves
1 cup / 197 grams vegetable oil
1 cup / 60 grams panko bread crumbs
3/4 teaspoon / 3 grams kosher salt

Method:

1. Preheat an oven to 375°F / 190°C.

2. Combine the garlic cloves and vegetable oil in a pot over medium-high heat.

3. Stirring constantly, bring the temperature of the oil to 375°F / 190°C. Once the oil reaches 375°F, maintain the temperature. Continue to fry the garlic until it is golden brown.

4. Once the garlic has browned, remove the oil from the heat and carefully strain off the oil. Discard the garlic. CAUTION: The oil will be extremely hot.

5. After the oil has cooled completely, mix the breadcrumbs with 1/4 cup / 50 grams of the garlic oil. Reserve the rest of the oil for another use.

6. Spread the breadcrumbs evenly on a sheet pan lined with parchment paper. Bake the breadcrumbs at 375°F / 190°C for approximately 8 minutes.

CARNE ASADA

We've all tasted carne asada that was too tough, cooked to the point where it might as well be called jerky. Cooking it sous vide not only tenderizes the skirt steak, it allows the marinade to deeply penetrate the fibers of the beef. Simply follow our recipe, grill briefly to finish and gild it with our vacuum-pickled escabeche for an added pop of spice and acidity.

Ingredients:

3 each / 15 grams garlic cloves
1 each / 73 grams jalapeño
1/4 cup / 11 grams cilantro
3 tablespoons / 38 grams tequila
1 each / 41 grams lime, juiced
1/4 cup / 44 grams extra virgin olive oil
1 tablespoon / 14 grams sherry vinegar
1.5 pounds / 680 grams skirt steak, not tenderized
vacuum-pickled escabeche as needed (see page 55)
smoked salsa roja as needed (see page 55)

Input data for Sous Vide Toolbox™

Units:	in / mm °F / °C
Protein:	Beef
Shape:	Steak
Thickness:	3/4 in / 19 mm
Cooking Method:	Cook and pasteurize to core
Desired Core Temperature:	134.6°F / 57°C
Initial Temperature:	41°F / 5°C
Water Temperature:	134.6°F / 57°C
Ice Bath:	Yes
Ice Bath Temperature:	33.8°F / 1°C
Final Food Temperature:	41°F / 5°C
Serves:	3

Calculated Times:

Cook Time:	18 hours, 1 minute
Tenderness Time:	17 hours
Cooling Time:	29 minutes
Total Time:	18 hours, 30 minutes plus 8 hours marinating time

Method:

1. Combine the garlic, jalapeño, cilantro, tequila, lime juice, olive oil and sherry vinegar in a blender and blend until smooth.

2. Place the skirt steak, along with the marinade in a vacuum pouch and vacuum-seal it. Refrigerate it for 8 hours.

3. Preheat a water bath to 134.6°F / 57°C.

4. Remove the skirt steak from the marinade and wipe off as much excess liquid as possible.

5. Vacuum-seal the skirt steak in a new vacuum pouch.

6. Place the vacuum pouch into the water bath, and cook it for 18 hours.

7. Carefully remove the vacuum pouch from the water bath and place it in a heavily iced bath.

8. Once the skirt steak has fully chilled, place the vacuum pouch in the refrigerator.

9. To serve the skirt steak, sear the skirt steak on both sides of the meat on a grill. Once you can see grill marks, move the steak to a cooler section of the grill to warm through. Slice the skirt steak against the grain and serve it with tortillas, smoked salsa roja and vacuum-pickled escabeche.

VACUUM-PICKLED ESCABECHE

Pickled vegetable escabeche is ubiquitous in most taquerias but can be made quickly and easily at home as well. You can reduce the amount of time it takes to pickle the vegetables to just a few hours by using a chamber vacuum sealer to brine your vegetables for you. You can use our method to pickle a wide variety of other vegetables as well, adding your own signature touch to classic dishes. Similar results can also be achieved by using an external vacuum sealer fitted with a canister.

Parameters:
Cook Time: 10 minutes
Yield: 6 1/2 cups

Ingredients:
4 each / 275 grams carrots, thinly sliced into rounds
5 each / 275 grams jalapeños, thinly sliced into rounds
2-1/2 cups / 275 grams cauliflower florets
1 cup / 264 grams simple syrup
1 cup / 210 grams white wine vinegar

Method:

1. Place the carrots, jalapeños and cauliflower in their own vacuum pouches.

2. Divide the simple syrup and vinegar evenly amongst the 3 vacuum pouches.

3. Seal the vacuum pouches in a chamber vacuum sealer. The vegetables will be ready to eat immediately. For best results, allow the flavor to mature overnight or up to a week before using.

4. When ready to serve, combine all of the vegetables and their liquids.

SMOKED SALSA ROJA

This update on a classic salsa recipe uses The Smoking Gun® to bring added depth and dimension, making it a great accompaniment to many dishes beyond traditional tortilla chips.

Parameters:
Cook Time: 25 minutes
Yield: 1 quart

Ingredients:
6 each / 32 grams dried pasilla peppers, stemmed, seeded
10 each / 7 grams dried chiles de arbol, stemmed, seeded
1 tablespoon / 11 grams kosher salt
1 teaspoon / 5 grams sugar
3 tablespoons / 41 grams white wine vinegar
5 each / 785 grams roma tomatoes, halved, charred
1 1/2 cups / 335 grams water
1/4 cup / 23 grams scallion, thinly sliced
1/4 cup / 11 grams cilantro, chopped

Special Equipment:
The Smoking Gun® handheld food smoker
PolyScience® Classic Smokehouse mesquite wood chips
Find more information at PolyScienceCulinary.com

Method:

1. Combine the pasilla peppers, chiles de arbol, salt, sugar, vinegar, tomatoes, water, scallions, and cilantro in a pot over medium high heat.

2. Crush the tomatoes so that they begin to release their juice.

3. Bring the mixture to a boil and continue to simmer it for approximately 15 to 20 minutes, until the mixture begins to thicken.

4. Remove the chiles from the mixture and add them to a blender with some of the cooking liquid. Blend until smooth.

5. Add the remaining ingredients and blend on low leaving the salsa slightly chunky.

6. Refrigerate the mixture until it is fully chilled.

7. Add the cilantro and scallions to the salsa and place it into a container with tight-fitting lid.

8. Insert the latex tube of The Smoking Gun® into the container and fill it with a dense smoke. Cover the container.

9. Allow the salsa to smoke for 5 minutes. Remove the lid and whisk the salsa. Repeat the smoking step.

POACHED RHUBARB

Poached rhubarb is one of those often-overlooked yet highly versatile creations that works wonders as a subtly sweet yet tart accent flavor. Add it to a puff pastry to create a unique tart. Use it as a topping for ice cream or yogurt. Fold it into whipped cream. The possibilities are truly endless — and delicious.

Parameters:

Thickness: 3/4 inch / 19 mm
Cook Time: 15 minutes
Temperature: 140°F / 60°C
Yield: 1 1/2 cups

Ingredients:

1/3 cup / 62 grams red wine vinegar
1/3 cup / 80 grams simple syrup
2 each / 237 grams rhubarb stalks

Method:

1. Preheat a water bath to 140°F / 60°C.

2. Combine all of the ingredients in a vacuum pouch and vacuum-seal it.

3. Place the vacuum pouch in the water bath and cook it for 15 minutes.

4. Place the vacuum pouch in a heavily iced bath.

5. Once the rhubarb has chilled thoroughly, strain off the liquid from the rhubarb and cut the rhubarb into bite-sized pieces. Reserve.

Poached rhubarb showcases one of the great benefits of sous vide cooking. Sous vide methods can maintain the original shape of fruits and vegetables while delivering the supple textures you want.

CAULIFLOWER SOUP

This is a vibrantly flavored chilled soup, perfect for a summer evening. It was created in our test kitchen and first served in our conference room with a group of international guests. They enjoyed the results so much they told us we had to share the recipe with the world. Consider this a promise kept.

Parameters:

Cook Time: 1 hour
Temperature: 185°F / 85°C
Yield: 4 1/2 cups

Ingredients:

3/4 each head of cauliflower, cut into florets
2 cups / 500 grams whole milk
1 tablespoon + 2 teaspoon / 15 grams kosher salt
1/8 cup / 27 grams simple syrup

Method:

1. Preheat a water bath to 185°F / 85°C.

2. Combine all of the ingredients in a vacuum pouch and vacuum-seal it.

3. Place the pouch in the preheated water bath and cook for 1 hour.

4. Remove the vacuum pouch and place it in a heavily iced bath.

5. After the pouch has chilled thoroughly, empty the contents into a blender and blend until smooth.

6. Strain the soup through a fine mesh sieve and serve.

DIVER SCALLOPS

Once you've tried double-cooked scallops, you'll have a difficult time enjoying them cooked any other way. Pre-cooking them allows you to set the interior texture exactly to your preference. Searing them afterward creates a firmer exterior and caramelized flavors that contrast beautifully with their tender interiors.

Ingredients:

2 cups / 500 grams water

2 tablespoons / 25 grams kosher salt

8 each / 296 grams diver scallops

2 tablespoons / 22 grams olive oil

rice bran, grape seed or other neutral-flavored oil with a high smoke point

2 tablespoons / 30 grams unsalted butter

4 each thyme sprigs

2 each garlic cloves, smashed

Input data for Sous Vide Toolbox™ (slow method)

Units:	in / mm °F / °C
Protein:	Shellfish
Shape:	Scallop
Thickness:	1 inch / 26 mm
Cooking Method:	Time to Temperature
Desired Core Temperature:	125°F / 51.6°C
Initial Temperature:	41°F / 5°C
Water Temperature:	125°F / 51.6°C
Ice Bath Temperature:	33.8°F / 1°C
Final Food Temperature:	41°F / 5°C
Serves:	4

Input data for Sous Vide Toolbox™ (fast method)

Units:	in / mm °F / °C
Protein:	Shellfish
Shape:	Scallop
Thickness:	1 inch / 26 mm
Cooking Method:	Time to Temperature
Core Temperature:	125°F / 51.6°C
Initial Temperature:	41°F / 5°C
Water Temperature:	126°F / 52.2°C
Ice Bath Temperature:	33.8°F / 1°C
Final Food Temperature:	41°F / 5°C
Serves:	4

Calculated Times:

Slow Method:	1 hour, 14 minutes	
	allow 10 minutes to brine	
Fast Method:	33 minutes	
	allow 10 minutes to brine	

Method:

1. Preheat water bath to 126°F / 52.2°C.

2. Combine the water and salt (an immersion hand blender or traditional stand mixer works well) in a non-reactive container, such as a glass or stainless steel mixing bowl.

3. Add the scallops to the saltwater mixture and allow them to brine for 10 minutes.

4. Remove the scallops from the brine and pat them completely dry with paper towels.

5. Place the scallops in a single layer in a vacuum pouch and vacuum-seal them. Take care not to crush the delicate scallops under the vacuum.

6. Place the vacuum pouch in the water bath and cook the scallops for 33 minutes.

7. Remove the vacuum pouch from the heated water bath and place it in a heavily iced bath.

8. To sear the scallops and re-therm them, heat a sauté pan over high heat. When you feel strong heat radiating from the pan, add a thin film of oil. When the oil begins to shimmer or look watery, carefully place the scallops in the pan while tilting the pan away from you to avoid the splatter of hot oil. When you begin to see a dark-brown color form around the bottom of the scallops and they have released themselves from the pan, flip them over.

9. Add the butter, thyme and garlic to the pan. Baste the browned tops of the scallops with the hot foamy butter, browning them further.

10. Remove the scallops from the pan and place them on a paper towel to rest for a moment. Plate and serve.

Using cold scallops allows you to sear them longer than if they were seared directly out of the heated water bath, producing a less pronounced gradient in texture. However, searing the scallops in advance also allows you to reduce the amount of time that the scallops need to remain in the water bath because they only need to be re-seared and lightly heated through.

In this recipe we are cooking 1°F / 0.6°C degree above our desired core temperature to firm the outer texture of the scallops because we like the differing texture gradient. Increasing the temperature is also a way to dramatically cut down on the cooking time while still delivering the supple results found in seafoods cooked at 125°F / 51.6°C.

RED AND GOLD BEETS

Beets are a misunderstood vegetable. Their reputation has been damaged by a lot of well-intentioned but misguided preparation methods. We promise that this recipe, however, will maximize the flavor, richness and reputation of your beets, wherever you choose to use them.

Parameters:

Thickness:	1 inch / 25 mm
Cook Time:	1 hour, 45 minutes
Temperature:	183.2°F / 84°C
Serves:	2 to 3

Ingredients:

3/4 pound / 340 grams small red and gold beets, tops removed, peeled, and halved (keep colors separate)

1/2 cup / 102 grams orange juice, divided

2 1/2 tablespoons / 23 grams lime juice, divided

1 each / 2 grams lime zest, divided

6 each / 0.2 grams black peppercorns, divided

2 tablespoons / 22 grams olive oil, divided

2 1/4 teaspoons / 9 grams kosher salt

Method:

1. Preheat water bath to 183.2°F / 84°C.

2. Segregating the two different colored beets, soak the two different groups in a mixture of orange juice, lime juice, lime zest, black peppercorns, olive oil and salt. Stir to coat evenly.

3. Place the beets, separated by color, and the other ingredients in two separate vacuum bags and vacuum-seal, taking care to keep everything in an even layer.

4. Place the vacuum pouches in the water bath and cook the beets for 1 hour and 45 minutes.

5. Remove the vacuum pouch from the water and open the pouch. Serve.

Cooking beets in an oven often requires probing and poking to test if they're done, which causes juices to seep out, creating a hard-to-clean mess and plenty of unpleasant aromas. Sous vide cooking makes the process foolproof and delivers that elusive crisp-tender texture that is so difficult to achieve using any other method.

LOBSTER ROLL

Preparing lobster can be a costly and time-consuming investment, but with sous vide cooking you can cook it perfectly with little effort. Here's a recipe that yields juicy and firm — but never rubbery — lobster every time.

Parameters:

Thickness:	13/16 inch / 20 mm
Cook Time:	30 minutes
Cooling Time:	15 minutes
Temperature:	140°F / 60°C
Serves:	3

Ingredients:

1 pound / 453 grams lobster tail, shelled

2 cups / 500 grams water

4 tablespoons / 50 grams kosher salt

2 tablespoons / 22 grams olive oil

1 each / 24 grams shallot, minced

1 tablespoon / 3 grams chive, thinly sliced

1/4 cup / 11 grams parsley, chopped

2 tablespoons / 28 grams mayonnaise

1/2 teaspoon / 2 grams sherry vinegar

1/2 each / 0.5 grams lemon, zested

kosher salt and black pepper to taste

3 New England-style hot dog buns, toasted

1 stalk celery, thinly sliced

vacuum-pickled red onion (see escabeche recipe on page 55 for method)

Method:

1. Preheat a water bath to 140°F / 60°C.

2. Using an immersion blender, combine the water and salt to make a brine. Once all of the salt has dissolved, add the lobster tails along with the brine to a food-safe container. Brine the lobster for 10 minutes.

3. Remove the tails from the brine and rinse them to wash off the excess brine.

4. Pat the lobster tails dry and place them in a vacuum pouch with 2 tablespoons / 22 grams of the olive oil and vacuum-seal them.

5. Place the lobster tails in the water bath and cook them for 30 minutes.

6. Remove the lobster tails from the bath and place the vacuum pouch in heavily iced water to chill thoroughly.

7. After the lobster has chilled thoroughly, dice the lobster tail into large chunks.

8. Combine the shallots, chives, parsley, mayonnaise, sherry vinegar, lemon zest, salt and pepper (to taste), in a mixing bowl and mix them well. After the dressing has been made, gently fold in the lobster.

9. Add the mixture to the hot dog buns and top with sliced celery and pickled onions.

DINNER

The first time I saw the sous vide technique, I was working in France. These cooks were taking whole chickens and putting them in bags with chicken stock and dropping them into a pot of water. After 30 minutes, they took the chickens out and finished them on the stove until they were golden brown.

I thought, "Wow! What the hell is going on?" I didn't understand what I'd witnessed because I had never seen it before. These guys explained to me what the process was. I didn't see sous vide used the rest of my time in France, but I had already begun to think of other uses and applications for it.

I came back to the U.S., and I still didn't see or hear of anyone doing it for several years, until I heard about Shea Gallante at Cru. He was using something called an immersion circulator, at which point I was reminded of my experience in France. And so I reached out to Dave Arnold to find me one of these contraptions. And Dave found Philip. And we've been making beautiful music together ever since.

Wylie Dufresne

Chef/Owner of Alder Restaurant and the iconic wd-50

NEW YORK STRIP STEAK

A well-cooked steak is an impressive thing to behold. Imagine cooking it to the perfect degree of doneness every time with absolute certitude.

Whether you're a kitchen novice or pro, following this recipe is an ideal way to become acquainted with the "Cooking Time to Temperature" technique that is fundamental to sous vide cooking. The common shape, thickness and texture of NY strip steaks provide a consistency that will allow you to learn about the sous vide process. And help you apply what you learned to other cuts of meat. The results are truly awe-inspiring. Once you quickly master the basics, you can expand your repertoire with different pre- and post-searing techniques and herb and spice combinations as well.

Ingredients:

13 ounce / 369 grams New York strip steak

1 tablespoon / 15 grams unsalted butter

3 thyme sprigs

kosher salt and cracked black pepper to taste

rice bran, grape seed or other neutral-flavored oil with a high smoke point

Input data for Sous Vide Toolbox™

Units:	in / mm °F / °C
Protein:	Beef
Shape:	Steak
Thickness:	1 1/4 inch / 31 mm
Cooking Method:	Time to Temperature
Desired Core Temperature:	137 °F / 58.3 °C
Initial Temperature:	41°F / 5 °C
Water Temperature:	137 °F / 58.3 °C
Tenderness Time:	None
Ice Bath:	None
Serves:	1

Calculated Time:

Cook Time: 2 hours, 19 minutes

Method:

1. Preheat the water bath to 137°F / 58.3°C.

2. Place the steak, butter and thyme in a vacuum pouch.

3. Vacuum-seal the pouch and place the steak in the circulating bath.

4. Once a core temperature of 137°F / 58.3°C has been reached, remove the bag from the bath. Remove the steak from the pouch and dry it with paper towels.

5. Heat a sauté pan over high heat. When you feel strong heat radiating from the pan, add a thin film of oil. When the oil begins to shimmer or look watery, carefully lay the steak in the pan. Once you begin to see a dark-brown color form around the bottom of the steak and it has released itself from the pan, flip the meat and sear the opposite side.

6. Remove the steak from the pan and allow it to rest for just a few moments before slicing, seasoning and plating.

Searing with grape seed oil, rice bran oil or another oil with a high smoke point (the temperature where it begins to burn) will reduce the amount of smoke generated. However, if you're cooking in a confined space with poor ventilation, pan searing may still produce too much smoke. A great sear can alternatively be created with the help of a torch or heat gun. These methods have their own pros and cons, but are much less prone to creating smoke. For further information on searing strategies, visit our blog post on this topic at PolyScienceCulinary.com.

Sous vide cooking provides multiple seasoning options. For example, adding salt to the surface of meat before cooking can create a dry or "cured" texture. Additionally, marinating meat in a water-salt brine attracts moisture and can be a great vehicle for additional flavors you may add. In most cases, however, we recommend seasoning with salt only after the sous vide process is complete because the salt can draw out too much moisture from the meat.

MASHED YUKON GOLD POTATOES

Mashed potatoes may be one of the world's most beloved comfort foods, but not all versions are created equal. We've all experienced less-than-stellar recipes, but we guarantee you that this sous vide version produces perfect results.

Simply vacuum-seal peeled and sliced potatoes in a pouch with salt and butter and place it in a sous vide water bath. In a few hours, the potatoes will be cooked to perfection and can be mashed right in the bag and kept warm in the water bath until you're ready to serve them. Like many other "side dishes," they can also be cooked and then refrigerated before being rewarmed as you prepare the rest of your meal, thus ensuring all your food will be served at the same time and temperature without any hassle. Our method frees up lots of time and energy and is ideal for entertaining.

Parameters:

Thickness:	3/8 inch / 9 mm
Cook Time:	3 hours
Temperature:	181.4°F / 83°C
Serves:	3

Ingredients:

1 pound / 453 grams Yukon Gold potatoes peeled and cut into approximately 3/8 inch / 9 mm-thick rounds

9 tablespoons / 135 grams unsalted butter

1/3 cup / 75 grams heavy whipping cream

5 each thyme sprigs

kosher salt and cracked black pepper to taste

Method:

1. Preheat the water bath to 181.4°F / 83°C.

2. Place the potatoes, butter, cream and thyme in a vacuum pouch.

3. Vacuum-seal the pouch and place it in the water bath for 3 hours.

4. Remove the vacuum pouch from the bath. Cut the bag open and pour the resulting liquid into a bowl.

5. Remove the thyme sprigs from the pouch and discard them. Rice the cooked potatoes through a potato ricer into the bowl containing the cooking liquid.

6. Gently combine the potatoes, butter and cream with a spatula.

7. Season the potato mixture with salt and black pepper. Serve.

Reheating potatoes or even just keeping them warm after cooking without scorching or drying them out can be difficult, but sous vide cooking makes it easy. To reheat potatoes, place them in a zip-top bag and clip it to the side of your water bath to warm.

For a chunky texture, carefully mash the potato mixture while it is still in the sealed bag and empty the contents into a serving bowl.

ASPARAGUS

It is often difficult to prepare perfectly cooked asparagus, especially when you are making several other items at the same time. Divert your attention elsewhere for just a few moments and the results are often mushy and waterlogged. Try to hurry through the process and you often get hard, undercooked spears. Fortunately, sous vide cooking makes it easy to produce uniformly satisfying textures without losing any flavor. Our recipe for asparagus pairs well with our New York strip and mashed potatoes, creating a perfectly balanced and downright irresistible sous vide meal.

Parameters:
Thickness: 5/16 inch / 8 mm
Cook Time: 4 minutes
Temperature: 194°F / 90°C
Serves: 2 to 3

Ingredients:
20 each / 453 grams asparagus
2 ounces / 60 grams olive oil
kosher salt to taste

Method:

1. Preheat the water bath to 194°F / 90°C.

2. Peel the asparagus and cut away any woody stems.

3. Place the asparagus and olive oil into a vacuum pouch and vacuum-seal it.

4. Place the asparagus pouch into the water bath and cook for 4 minutes.

5. Remove the asparagus from the bath and cut the bag open. Season the asparagus with salt and serve immediately.

If you are cooking the asparagus in advance, plunge the spears directly into a heavily iced bath immediately after heating to stop the cooking process. To warm them, pre-heat a sauté pan over high heat. When you feel a strong heat coming from the pan, empty the spears into the pan and sauté them until they are just warmed through.

You can sous vide all your vegetable for the entire week at one time. Simply chill each individual pouch in a water bath immediately after cooking and refrigerate. They will typically be cooked at higher temperatures than proteins. However, the cooking temperature for most proteins is adequate for rewarming and then serving. So simply add the vegetables to the bath in which proteins are cooking to conveniently create an entire meal whenever you want it.

CORN SOUP

There are many advantages to cooking corn soup sous vide as opposed to using more traditional methods. For example, the sous vide process allows you to easily "step cook" the corn, increasing the temperature of the bath part way through cooking in order to augment the sweetness and flavor of the corn. The sous vide method ensures things don't get messy while eliminating the possibility of scorching the soup.

Parameters:
Cook Time: 1 hour, 10 minutes + time to increase bath temperature
Temperature: 167°F / 75°C - 185°F / 85°C
Yield: 1 quart

Ingredients:
8 each / 1728 grams corn on the cob
1 pound / 453 grams frozen corn kernels
1/3 cup / 80 grams simple syrup
1 tablespoon + 2 teaspoons / 15 grams kosher salt
1 1/2 teaspoons / 7 grams sherry vinegar
bacon-shallot jam, as needed

Method:

1. Preheat a water bath to 167°F / 75°C.

2. Cut the corn kernels from the cobs and juice them using a masticating juicer. This should yield approximately 2 1/2 cups / 654 grams of corn juice. Discard the pulp.

3. Divide the unstrained corn juice, corn kernels, salt and simple syrup evenly between two vacuum pouches.

4. Vacuum-seal the pouches and cook them in the water bath at 167°F / 75°C for 1 hour.

5. Increase the bath temperature to 185°F / 85°C. Once the bath reaches this temperature, continue to cook for an additional 10 minutes.

6. Carefully remove the pouches from the water bath and pour the contents into a blender. Blend the soup until it is smooth and season it with the sherry vinegar.

7. Strain the soup through a fine-mesh sieve.

8. To serve, garnish the soup with bacon-shallot jam.

BACON-SHALLOT JAM

We love bacon and try to include it in as many dishes as we can. Our bacon-shallot jam is a stand-alone condiment that allows you to add as much bacon flavor as you'd like to any dish in your repertoire. The combination of pork, caramelized shallots, thyme and sweet maple syrup meld with the pleasant bite of the sherry vinegar to create a nuanced smoky-sweet spread.

Parameters:
Cook Time: 15 minutes
Yield: 1 cup

Ingredients:
1 1/2 cups / 230 grams bacon, medium dice
1 3/4 cups / 178 grams shallot, thinly sliced
3 each thyme sprigs
4 tablespoons / 56 grams sherry vinegar
1/3 cup / 117 grams maple syrup

Method:

1. Preheat a sauté pan over medium-high heat. Once you begin to feel a strong heat radiating from the pan, add the bacon. Render the bacon completely.

2. Once the bacon is crispy, remove it from the pan and reserve. Add the shallots and thyme to the bacon fat. Cook the shallots in the bacon fat until they begin to brown.

3. Deglaze the pan with all but 1 1/2 teaspoons / 7 grams of the sherry vinegar. Reduce the sherry vinegar completely.

4. Discard the thyme. Add the maple syrup and bacon to the pan.

5. Reduce the maple syrup until it glazes the bacon and shallots.

6. Stir in the remaining 1 1/2 teaspoons / 7 grams of sherry vinegar. Reserve.

You should also try combining the bacon jam with our French toast recipe on page 43. The combination is wonderful.

72-HOUR SHORT RIBS

Preparing perfectly cooked short ribs, which are both tender and juicy, is a rare achievement. It's well known how gently cooking "low and slow" can transform secondary cuts of meat into culinary stars, but sous vide allows you to maintain the exact level of doneness you desire while still enjoying the tenderizing benefits of braising. It's easy, for example, to serve medium-rare ribs and other cuts of meat that are incredibly tender, as you'll quickly find with this richly flavorful offering.

Ingredients:

1 pound, 10 1/2 ounces / 750 grams / 4 bone-in beef short ribs

8 cups / 1890 grams water

1/4 cup / 41 grams kosher salt

rice bran, grape seed or other neutral-flavored oil with a high smoke point

2 tablespoons / 30 grams unsalted butter

4 each thyme sprigs

2 each crushed garlic cloves

sea salt and cracked black pepper to taste

Input data for Sous Vide Toolbox™

Units:	in / mm °F / °C
Protein:	Beef
Shape:	Short Rib Squares
Thickness:	1 1/2 inch / 38 mm
Cooking Method:	Cook and Pasteurize Surface
Desired Core Temperature:	135°F / 57.2°C
Initial Temperature:	41°F / 5°C
Water Temperature:	135°F / 57.2°C
Ice Bath:	On
Ice Bath Temperature:	33.8°F / 1°C
Final Food Temperature:	41°F / 5°C
Serves:	2

Calculated Times:

Cook Time:	72 hours, 2 minutes
Tenderness Time:	70 hours, 45 minutes
Cooling Time:	37 minutes
Total Time:	72 hours, 39 minutes

Method:

1. Combine the water and salt in immersion blender or stand mixer. Once all of the salt has dissolved, add the short ribs and salt solution to a food-safe container and brine for 24 hours.

2. Preheat the water bath to 135°F / 57.2°C.

3. Remove the short ribs from the brine and dry them well with paper towels.

4. Heat a sauté pan over high heat. When you feel strong heat radiating from the pan, add a thin film of oil to the pan. When the oil begins to "shimmer" or look watery, carefully lay the short ribs in the pan. Once you begin to see a dark-brown color form around the bottom of the ribs and they have released themselves from the pan, remove them.

5. Place the seared short ribs in a vacuum pouch. Without sealing it, plunge the bag into a heavily iced bath for 15 minutes with the top of the pouch clipped to the side of the bath.

6. Vacuum-seal the short ribs and place them in the water bath. Cook the short ribs for 72 hours. They will be tender after 48 hours but become meltingly supple after 72 hours.

7. Remove the short ribs from the water bath and plunge them into a heavily iced bath until thoroughly cooled.

8. To warm the short ribs, heat them in a water bath set to 133°F / 56.1°C for 40 minutes.

9. The short ribs may be served "as is" or may be re-seared to refresh the crust and boost flavor. When re-searing the short ribs, add the thyme, garlic and butter to the pan. Basting the short ribs with the hot foamy butter will aid in deepening the color and enriching the ribs' natural aroma.

When buying cuts of meat that require some trimming, don't throw anything away. There are several useful ways to use those trimmings. For example, after searing the trimmings to a deep dark-brown, you can add them to a sous vide pouch, creating a umami bomb of rich flavor. Another idea that we've learned from our friends Aki Kamozowa and Alex Talbot of IdeasInFood.com is to take those seared trimmings, deglaze the pan and add everything to a pressure cooker for 30 minutes with a flavorful liquid. You can reduce the liquid into a thick gravy and use it as a finishing sauce for your short ribs.

After cooking the short ribs for 24 hours at 131°F / 55°C, collagen will begin to become tender. You can increase the tenderness by increasing the cook time. Alternatively, you may decrease the cook time and increase the temperature. For example, cooking short ribs at 144°F / 62°C for 48 hours will also produce a great result.

CUMIN BUTTER CARROTS

You won't lose any color, flavor or aroma when cooking vegetables sous vide. Everything stays in the bag. These cumin butter carrots provide a perfect balance of earthiness, spice and a deep, satisfying richness.

Parameters:

Thickness: 5/8 inch / 16 mm
Cook Time: 1 hour
Temperature: 183.2°F / 84°C
Serves: 2

Ingredients:

12 each / 204 grams baby carrots
2 tablespoons / 30 grams unsalted butter
1/2 tablespoon / 7 grams cumin
salt to taste

Method:

1. Pre-heat the water bath to 183.2°F / 84°C.

2. Place all of the ingredients into a vacuum pouch, making sure that all of the ingredients are laid flat in a single layer and not clustered as a bunch.

3. Vacuum-seal the pouch using a high vacuum setting. If your chamber vacuum sealer allows it, pull 10 seconds of extra vacuum. This extra vacuum will help to remove air that is embedded within the carrots and help keep them from floating in the bath.

4. Place the vacuum pouch into the water bath. After the butter has fully melted, carefully lift the bag out of the bath and gently massage it to evenly distribute the seasoning. Return the bag to the bath and continue to cook until the carrots are tender.

5. Once the carrots are tender, simply cut the bag open and serve.

BRUSSELS SPROUTS

In order to make crispy caramelized Brussels sprouts, you need to dry them out and apply a strong sear. Steaming or boiling them allows the sprouts to take on too much water, but sous vide keeps things relatively dry, providing an opportunity to properly brown them on the stove.

Parameters:

Thickness: 9/16 inch / 15 mm
Cook Time: 4 minutes
Temperature: 194°F / 90°C
Serves: 2

Ingredients:

15 each / 410 grams Brussels sprouts
2 tablespoons / 22 grams olive oil
kosher salt, cracked black pepper, and lemon juice to taste

Method:

1. Preheat your water bath to 194°F / 90°C.

2. Place the Brussels sprouts and oil into a vacuum pouch in one even layer and vacuum-seal.

3. Place the vacuum-sealed pouch into the preheated bath and cook for 4 minutes. Brussels sprouts may outgas during cooking and are inclined to float. If necessary, weigh it down with a plate or saucer.

4. While the Brussels sprouts are cooking sous vide, preheat a sauté pan or cast iron skillet over medium-high heat. This will be used to sear the Brussels sprouts after they have been cooked sous vide.

5. Remove the Brussels sprouts from the water and cut the bag open immediately. Add the Brussels sprouts to the preheated pan and turn the heat up to high. Sauté the sprouts until they begin to brown slightly and add the lemon juice. Season them to taste with salt and black pepper.

6. Remove the Brussels sprouts from the pan and place them on a paper towel to drain off any excess oil and lemon juice. Serve immediately.

Vegetables of the brassica family — such as broccoli, Brussels sprouts and kale — release pungent aromas during the blanching process. To prevent this process from taking place, rapidly chill the vegetables in a heavily iced bath after cooking and cut the bag open only after the vegetables are completely cooled. You can then store them in a lidded container without fear of unwanted smells.

Pectin is the "glue" that holds fruits and vegetables together. It begins to break down at 185°F / 85°C. By cooking just under that temperature, you can tenderize fruits and vegetables without destroying the pectin and making them mushy. Conversely, if you are cooking the fruits or vegetables to make a puree, aim for 185°F / 85°C or higher.

RIB RUB

These are two recipes that can help make many of your kitchen creations even more flavorful and vibrant. Again, we urge you to try different combinations in order for you to find your favorite balance of ingredients and flavor.

Parameters:

Cook Time: 5 minutes

Yield: 1/2 cups

Ingredients:

1/2 cup / 125 grams packed brown sugar

1 tablespoon / 10 grams kosher salt

1 tablespoon / 9 grams black pepper, cracked

2 teaspoons / 7 grams chili powder

2 teaspoons / 7 grams smoked paprika

1 teaspoon / 4 grams garlic powder

1 teaspoon / 3 grams mustard powder

1/4 teaspoon / 1 gram piment d'espellete

Method:

1. Combine all of the ingredients and mix well. Reserve.

MUSTARD BARBECUE SAUCE

Parameters:

Cook Time: 15 minutes

Yield: 2 cups

Ingredients:

1 cup / 300 grams whole grain mustard

3/4 cup / 126 grams apple cider

1/8 cup / 30 grams white wine vinegar

1/8 cup / 30 grams ketchup

1 tablespoon / 15 grams brown sugar

1 tablespoon / 10 grams worcestershire

1/2 teaspoon / 1.5 grams black pepper

1 1/2 teaspoons / 6 grams kosher salt

1 teaspoon / 4 grams garlic powder

1 teaspoon / 2.5 grams smoked paprika

1/4 teaspoon / 1 grams cayenne

Method:

1. Combine all of the ingredients in a pot over medium high heat.

2. Stirring constantly, bring the mixture to a boil.

3. Once the mixture has come to a boil, remove the pot from the heat and allow it to cool completely. Reserve.

BABY BACK RIBS

Traditional cooking methods often call for high temperatures to tenderize, but the results are often dry. Cooking ribs sous vide in sealed packages allows the meat to cook low and slow while retaining its juices. In this recipe, ribs can be cooked well ahead of time and chilled. Just pull them from the fridge and briefly broil whenever you want to create an outstanding meal. Nothing could be more convenient and delicious.

Ingredients:
2 lb. / 906 grams pork baby back ribs
rib rub (see recipe on page 73)
mustard barbecue sauce (see recipe on page 73)

Input data for Sous Vide Toolbox™

Units:	in / mm °F / °C
Protein:	Pork
Shape:	Rib Rack with Bones
Thickness:	13/16 inch / 20 mm
Cooking Method:	Cook and Pasteurize Core
Desired Core Temperature:	145°F / 62.8°C
Initial Temperature:	41°F / 5°C
Water Temperature:	145°F / 62.8°C
Ice Bath:	On
Ice Bath Temperature:	33.8°F / 1°C
Final Food Temperature:	41°F / 5°C
Serves:	2 to 3

Calculated Times:

Cook Time:	24 hours, 5 minutes
Tenderness Time:	23 hours
Cooling Time:	32 minutes
Total Time:	24 hours, 37 minutes

Method:

1. Preheat a water bath to 145°F / 62.8°C.

2. Coat the ribs evenly and thoroughly with the rib rub.

3. Place the ribs in a vacuum pouch and vacuum-seal it.

4. Place the vacuum pouch in the preheated water bath and cook the ribs for 24 hours.

5. Remove the ribs from the water bath and place the vacuum pouch in a heavily iced bath.

6. After the ribs have chilled thoroughly, transfer them to the refrigerator until ready to use.

7. To serve, brush the ribs with the barbecue sauce and sear them under a broiler until heated through.

8. Apply another coat of barbecue sauce and lightly dust the ribs with rib rub. Serve.

CORN ON THE COB

Most people are skeptical about cooking corn on the cob sous vide until they taste the results. The truth of the matter is traditional cooking methods often yield overcooked or undercooked corn, but sous vide delivers exceptional results while providing you great flexibility in your kitchen. There's no need to watch over a pot or grill, so focus on the rest of the meal and come back to the corn at your convenience. It will be ready when you are.

Parameters:
Thickness:	1 7/8 inch / 47 mm
Cook Time:	30 minutes
Temperature:	180°F / 82.2°C
Serves:	4

Ingredients:
4 each / 753 grams corn on the cob
3 tablespoons / 45 grams unsalted butter
kosher salt to taste

Method:

1. Preheat a water bath to 180°F / 82.2°C.

2. Combine the corn and butter in a vacuum pouch and vacuum-seal it.

3. Place the vacuum pouch in the water bath and cook it for 30 minutes.

4. Remove the corn from the vacuum pouch.

5. Season the corn with salt. Serve.

POACHED SALMON

Cooking fish is a great way to explore how textures can be manipulated through sous vide cooking. It's easy, for example, to create seafood offerings with crispy skin and silky interiors. Boiling salmon in its sous vide pouch for just a minute will slightly firm up the exterior of the fish while pasteurizing it, creating a seafood delicacy that's as supple as it is safe to eat.

Ingredients:

5 1/4 cups / 1,250 grams water

3/4 cup / 125 grams kosher salt

2 each / 0.34 lb. / 155 grams salmon filets, skinned (310 grams total)

2 tablespoons / 22 grams olive oil

sea salt to taste

cannellini bean soup (see page 79)

celery root (see page 78)

Input data for Sous Vide Toolbox™

Units:	in / mm °F / °C
Protein:	Fatty Fish
Shape:	Filet
Thickness:	1 1/16 inch / 27 mm
Cooking Method:	Time to Temperature
Desired Core Temperature:	128°F / 53.3°C
Initial Temperature:	41°F / 5°C
Water Temperature:	132.8°F / 56°C
Serves:	2

Calculated Time:

Cook Time: 49 minutes

allow 10 minutes to brine

Method:

1. Preheat a water bath to 132.8°F / 56°C.

2. Bring a pot of water to a strong rolling boil on the stove. (Make sure that the pot is large enough to accommodate the pouch that you will be using for the salmon.)

3. Combine the water and salt in a non-reactive container made of glass, stainless steel or plastic. (An immersion or stand blender is helpful.)

4. Add the salmon to the salt water mixture and brine for 10 minutes.

5. Remove the salmon filets from the brine and rinse off the excess brine under cold running water. Pat the filets completely dry with paper towels.

6. Combine the salmon with the olive oil in a vacuum pouch and vacuum-seal. Take care to keep the salmon in one layer and not to crush the delicate fish filets.

7. Place the salmon pouch into the boiling water and boil it for 1 minute.

8. Remove the pouch from the boiling water and place it into the pre-heated water bath.

9. Cook sous vide for 49 minutes.

10. Remove the vacuum pouch from the water bath and carefully cut the pouch open. Season the salmon with sea salt and serve with cannellini bean soup and celery root.

Brining seafood serves two key purposes in addition to just adding seasoning. First, the brining will denature albumen proteins on the exterior of the seafood and prevent it from taking on a milky appearance as it cooks. Secondly, brining the seafood will slightly firm up its texture.

CELERY ROOT

In this recipe, the humble celery root is prepared as if it were a scallop, creating a unique texture and flavor to a simple root vegetable. We think it adds an interesting twist to any meal. You be the judge.

Parameters:

Thickness: 7/8 inch / 22 mm
Cook Time: 2 hours, 30 minutes
Temperature: 147.2°F / 64°C
Serves: 2

Ingredients:

1 each celery root, peeled and sliced into 7/8 inch / 22 mm rounds
2 tablespoons / 22 grams olive oil
kosher salt and cracked black pepper to taste

Method:

1. Preheat a water bath to 147.2°F / 64°C.

2. Combine the celery root with the olive oil in a vacuum pouch and vacuum-seal it, taking care to keep the celery root in an even layer.

3. Place the vacuum pouch in the water bath and cook for 2 hours and 30 minutes.

4. Remove the pouch from the water bath and place it in a heavily iced bath until it has chilled completely.

5. Remove the celery root from the package and cut it into your desired shape.

6. To sear the celery root, heat a sauté pan over high heat. When you feel a strong heat radiating from the pan, add a thin film of oil to the pan. When the oil begins to shimmer or look watery, carefully place the celery root in the pan. Once you begin to see a dark-brown color form around the bottom of the slices and they have released themselves from the pan, flip the them over.

7. After the opposite side has developed a nice sear, place the celery root pieces on a paper towel to drain off any excess oil.

8. Season to taste with kosher salt and black pepper. Serve.

Cooking root vegetables sous vide ahead of time is a great way to prepare your meals for the entire week. For example, it only takes about 30 minutes to rewarm carrots once they are thoroughly cooked and chilled. When your protein is cooking or warming, simply drop your vegetables in the same water bath during the last 30 minutes of the cooking process to make sure everything is ready to be served at the same time. For more perspectives on cooking vegetables, see Bruno Goussault's comments about cooling and re-therming on pages 30-31.

CANNELLINI BEAN SOUP

Cooking beans sous vide produces perfect results every time without watching over a pot, or even the need for a pot! Of course, they can be served whole, pureed for a creamier texture, or cooked to yield a texture anywhere in between. In this case, the beans are served as a garnish for the salmon. Of course, they can also be served as a stand-alone soup.

Parameters:

Thickness: N/A
Cook Time: 2 hours, 30 minutes
Temperature: 194°F / 90°C
Serves: 4 to 6

Ingredients:

1/2 each / 155 grams onion, small diced

grape seed oil

1 pound / 453 grams cannellini beans, soaked overnight, divided

4 cups / 900 grams vegetable stock or water, divided

2 each garlic cloves, divided

2 each thyme sprigs, divided

2 each bay leaves, divided

1 tablespoon / 12 grams kosher salt

1 teaspoon / 7 grams champagne vinegar

Method:

1. Preheat the water bath to 194°F / 90°C.

2. Heat a sauté pan over medium heat. When you feel a strong heat radiating from the pan, add enough oil to the pan to coat the bottom with a thin film.

3. Add the onions to the pan and sweat them over medium heat until they become translucent. Remove the onions from the pan and chill them completely.

4. Combine the onions, beans, vegetable stock, garlic, thyme, and bay leaves and then split the mixture evenly into two vacuum-seal pouches.

5. Vacuum-seal the pouches, and cook the beans for 2 hours and 30 minutes.

6. Carefully cut the vacuum pouches open and remove the thyme and bay leaves.

7. Strain the solids out from the cooking liquid. Measure out 2 3/4 cups / 640 grams of the cooking liquid and reserve. Hold the rest of the liquid off to the side in case you want to thin the consistency of the soup further.

8. Puree the onions and beans with the reserved cooking liquid and season with the kosher salt and champagne vinegar.

9. Pass the puree through a fine mesh sieve and reserve. Serve as soup, sauce or garnish.

Avoid "Thyme Bombs." Cooking food in vacuum-sealed pouches locks in all the flavors of the ingredients. Nothing escapes. Therefore, most sous vide recipes call for a reduction in the amount of spices, herbs and other flavorings that you would normally use. The amount of salt that is required, however, usually remains the same.

If you are making the soup ahead of time, you may hold the soup warm in a water bath set to 165°F / 73.9°C.

PHILIP'S THANKSGIVING DINNER

Thanksgiving dinner can be one of the most challenging meals to cook, requiring multiple cooking methods and a variety of side dishes. Over the years, I have developed a method for cooking the entire Thanksgiving meal by way of sous vide. There are a few finishing touches, such as deep frying the turkey that may require some effort and special equipment, but by utilizing the sous vide method, you can devote plenty of attention to these finishing touches. The sous vide water bath will take on the majority of the workload and allow you a very pleasant cooking experience, one that may even allow you to entertain your guests instead of tending to the stove all day.

WHITE & DARK TURKEY MEAT

Over the years, I've found that most of my guests at holiday meals prefer the white meat of our turkey. This recipe has transformed them into dark-meat fans. In fact, it's sometimes all I cook because the dark meat has become so popular.

Ingredients:

1 1/2 gallons / 5,430 grams water
3/4 cup / 123 grams kosher salt
2 each / 662 gram turkey drumsticks
2 each / 1,215 gram turkey thighs
2 each / 1,200 gram turkey breasts
2 cups / 720 grams spiced duck fat (see page 82)
kosher salt to taste

Input data for Sous Vide Toolbox™

Units:	in / mm °F / °C
Temperature:	132.8°F / 56°C
Protein:	Poultry
Shape:	Whole Thigh / Leg
Thickness:	Thigh 2-3/8 in / 60 mm
	Breast 2-1/4 in / 57 mm
Cooking Method:	Cook and Pasteurize to core
Desired Core Temperature:	149°F / 65°C
Initial Temperature:	41°F / 5°C
Water Temperature:	149°F / 65°C
Ice Bath	On
Ice Bath Temperature	33.8°F / 1°C
Final Food Temperature:	41°F / 5°C
Serves:	3

Calculated Times:

Cook Time:	Thighs:	7 hours, 58 minutes
	Breasts:	3 hours, 48 minutes
Cooling Time:		3 hours, 8 minutes
Total Time:		11 hours, 6 minutes
		allow 24 hours to brine

Method:

1. With an immersion blender, combine the water and salt. Once all of the salt has dissolved, add the turkey pieces and brine to a food-safe container and brine for 24 hours.

2. Place your immersion circulator in your desired cooking vessel and preheat the water bath to 149°F / 65°C.

3. Remove the turkey pieces from the brine and wrap them in paper towels until they are completely dry. (This may take several attempts.)

4. Pair the legs in a vacuum pouch and place each thigh and breast in its own vacuum pouch. Evenly divide the duck fat into each of the 5 vacuum pouches. Vacuum-seal the pouches. Refrigerate the turkey breasts.

5. Place the thigh and leg pouches in a preheated water bath and cook them for 4 hours and 10 minutes. At this time, add the turkey breasts to the water bath and continue to cook for another 3 hours and 48 minutes.

6. After a total of 8 hours has elapsed, remove the vacuum pouches from the water bath and place them into a heavily iced bath to chill thoroughly.

7. To serve, preheat a fryer to 375°F / 190°C. Once the fryer is up to temperature, fry the drumsticks for 4 minutes, thighs for 9 minutes, and breasts for 8 minutes. Drain the turkey pieces on paper towels and season them with salt. Serve.

SPICED DUCK FAT

Duck fat is heavenly. We thought that the deep richness couldn't be topped, but we've found a way to make it even more decadent. Adding spices while extracting and mellowing the flavor of the duck fat through sous vide cooking produces a wonderful condiment that can elevate some of your best dishes to even greater heights.

Parameters:
Cook Time: 20 minutes
Temperature: 185°F / 85°C
Yield: 2 cups

Ingredients:
1 each / 4 grams cinnamon stick
4 each / 3.5 grams whole star anise
1/2 teaspoon / 1.5 grams juniper berries
1 tablespoon + 1 teaspoon / 7.5 grams ground green cardamom
1 teaspoon / 2.3 grams ground allspice
1 teaspoon / 3 grams ground clove
2 cups / 392 grams duck fat

Method:

1. Preheat a water bath to 185°F / 85°C.

2. Toast the cinnamon, star anise and juniper berries over medium-low heat until they become fragrant.

3. Add the toasted spices to a spice grinder and grind them into a fine powder. Strain the spice powder through a fine mesh sieve. Discard the solids left in the strainer.

4. In a vacuum pouch, combine all of the ingredients and vacuum-seal it.

5. Place the pouch into the preheated water bath and cook it for 20 minutes.

6. Remove the pouch and place it in a heavily iced bath to chill thoroughly. Reserve.

SMASHED SWEET POTATOES

The sous vide method allows easy "step cooking" of foods at varied temperatures. This technique is a great way to make sweet potatoes even sweeter and more flavorful without adding sugar or other flavorings.

Parameters:
Thickness: 1 inch / 25 mm
Cook Time: 3 hours, 35 minutes + time to increase bath temperature
Temperature: 153°F / 67.2°C - 185°F / 85°C
Serves: 2 to 4

Ingredients:
2 each / 858 grams sweet potatoes
2 tablespoons / 30 grams unsalted butter
3 tablespoons / 29 grams maple syrup
1 teaspoon / 1 gram nutmeg
1 teaspoon / 3 grams cinnamon
2 tablespoons / 8.5 grams kosher salt

Method:

1. Preheat a water bath to 153°F / 67.2°C.

2. Peel the sweet potatoes and cut them into 1 inch / 2.5 cm slices. Combine all of the ingredients in a vacuum pouch, making sure to keep the sweet potatoes in one even layer, and vacuum-seal.

3. Place the vacuum pouch in the water bath and cook for 2 hours.

4. Increase the bath temperature to 185°F / 85°C.

5. Once the water bath has reached 185°F / 85°C, cook the sweet potatoes for another hour and 35 minutes.

6. Carefully remove the sweet potatoes from the water bath and place the pouch on a flat surface.

7. Place a dry cloth towel on top of the bag and mash the sweet potatoes in the bag to your desired texture and serve.

Step cooking the sweet potatoes allows the starches in the sweet potatoes to convert to sugar. The process is called saccharification and generally takes place between 131°F / 55°C and 162°F / 72.2°C. The two enzymes responsible for the changes are alpha amylase and beta amylase. Although each are active between different temperature ranges, a good compromise between the two is 153°F / 67.2°C.

CREAMY POLENTA WITH WILD MUSHROOMS

Polenta makes a great side dish. It can also be served as a "middle of the plate" gluten-free base flavor for vegetarian, meat, poultry or seafood entreés. And as an added bonus, no constant stirring over a hot stove is required with this sous vide recipe.

Parameters:

Cook Time:	2 hours
Temperature:	194°F / 90°C
Serves:	2 to 3

Ingredients:

3/4 cup / 125 grams coarse ground polenta

2 cups / 500 grams vegetable stock or water

1 1/2 cup / 42 grams parmigiano reggiano, freshly grated

grape seed or other neutral, high smoke point oil

1 pound / 453 grams mushrooms

4 tablespoons / 46 grams shallots, minced

4 each / 16 grams garlic cloves, minced

1/2 cup / 125 grams white wine

1/2 cup / 125 grams vegetable stock

2 tablespoons / 3 grams fresh tarragon, chopped

kosher salt, black pepper and sherry vinegar to taste

4 tablespoons / 60 grams unsalted butter, softened

1/3 cup / 76 grams mascarpone cheese, softened

Method:

1. Preheat a water bath to 194°F / 90°C.

2. Combine the polenta and vegetable stock in a vacuum pouch and vacuum-seal it.

3. Cook the polenta for 120 minutes until the liquid is fully absorbed and the polenta is tender. Carefully massage the bag every 20 minutes.

4. Heat a sauté pan over high heat. When you feel strong heat radiating from the pan, add a thin film of oil. When the oil begins to shimmer or look watery, carefully add the mushrooms. In order to develop a strong caramelization, it is important to leave the mushrooms alone because stirring or shaking will cause them to steam and resist browning. Once you begin to see a dark brown color form around the bottom of the mushrooms, you may move them.

5. When mushrooms have browned evenly, add the shallots and garlic. Sweat them, taking care not to brown the shallots and garlic. Deglaze the pan by adding white wine and reduce it by half. Add the stock and reduce the liquid in the pan until it just glazes the mushrooms.

6. Season the mushrooms with salt, black pepper, and sherry vinegar. Add the tarragon and remove the pan from the heat.

7. Carefully remove the bag of polenta from the water bath. Open the bag and pour the polenta into a serving bowl. Gently stir in the cheeses and softened butter. Top with the sautéed mushrooms. Serve or hold warm in a zip-top bag clipped to the side of your bath.

Sous vide is a convenient method for making great polenta; however, it's important to note that polenta does not reheat well. So plan to enjoy it as soon as it's cooked.

DOUBLE-CUT PORK CHOPS

A great pork chop can be one of life's simple but great culinary pleasures. Unfortunately, most of us are used to eating overcooked pork. That's especially the case with double cuts because traditional cooking methods often dry them out on the outside before they are adequately cooked on the inside. By following this recipe, you'll be learning ideas that apply to other cuts of meat, all while producing a one-of-a-kind pork chop dinner.

Ingredients:

1 each 32 oz / 907 grams double-cut pork chop
1 gallon / 3,780 grams water
1/2 cup / 82 grams kosher salt
2 tablespoons / 22 grams olive oil
1 each / 3 grams strip of lemon zest
2 each thyme sprigs
2 each rosemary sprigs
2 each sage leaves
sea salt and cracked black pepper to taste

Input data for Sous Vide Toolbox™ (slow method)

Units:	in / mm °F / °C
Protein:	Pork
Shape:	Chop
Thickness:	2 inch / 51 mm
Cooking Method:	Cook and Pasteurize to Core
Desired Core Temperature:	145°F / 62.7°C
Initial Temperature:	41°F / 5°C
Water Temperature:	145°F / 62.7°C

Input data for Sous Vide Toolbox™ (fast method)

Units:	in / mm °F / °C
Protein:	Pork
Shape:	Chop
Thickness:	2 inch / 51 mm
Cooking Method:	Cook and Pasteurize to Core
Desired Core Temperature:	145°F / 62.7°C
Initial Temperature:	41°F / 5°C
Water Temperature:	146°F / 63.3°C

Calculated Times:

Slow Method:	5 hours, 10 minutes
	allow 24 hours to brine
Fast Method:	3 hours, 26 minutes
	allow 24 hours to brine

Method:

1. Mix the salt and water together using an immersion blender or stand mixer. Add the pork chops and salt water mixture to a food-safe container and brine for 24 hours.

2. Preheat a water bath to 145°F / 62.7°C (slow method) or 146°F / 63.3°C (fast method).

3. Remove the pork chops from the brine and completely dry them with paper towels. (This may take several attempts.)

4. Place the pork chops, lemon zest, olive oil, thyme, rosemary and sage in a vacuum pouch. Vacuum-seal the pouch.

5. Place the pouch into the preheated water bath and cook it for 5 hours and 10 minutes (slow method) or 3 hours and 26 minutes (fast method).

6. Remove the pork chops from the water bath once the core temperature has been reached. Cut the vacuum pouch open and again dry the surface of the chops completely with paper towels.

7. Heat a sauté pan over high heat. When you feel strong heat radiating from the pan, add a thin film of oil. When the oil begins to shimmer or look watery, carefully lay the pork chop in the pan while tilting the pan away from you to avoid the splatter of hot oil. Once you begin to see a dark-brown color form around the bottom of the chop and it has released itself from the pan, flip and sear the opposite side.

8. When the pork chop has been seared on both sides, allow it to rest for 1 minute before slicing. Serve.

Increasing thickness of foods will increase their cook times exponentially. In fact a "4X" time difference is not uncommon for what may seem to be slight differences in dimension. So, what can you do if you don't want to wait 5 hours for your pork chop? Raise your bath 1-2°F / 1°C above your target core temp and probe the pork chop as it cooks so that you can stop the process at the moment you reach the desired core temperature of 145°F / 62.7°C. To accomplish this precision, apply a 3/4-inch piece of high density foam tape to the outside of the pouch and insert a hypodermic thermocouple type probe into the food. Make sure that the tip of the probe is at the very center of the thickest part of whatever you are cooking. The probe will indicate the exact moment the cooking should stop. Utilizing this method, you may see some "overcook" around the edges, yielding a more traditional gradient in temperature and textural doneness to the meat.

One way to get a perfect sear on the exterior of oddly shaped cuts is to "cryo-fry" them. We first learned about this method from our friends at *Modernist Cuisine*. Cryo-frying benefits sous vide foods because it produces virtually no "overcook" during the searing step. During the process, food is dipped in liquid nitrogen for 30 seconds and then immediately transferred to a fryer preheated to 350°F / 176.6°C for 40 seconds. Not only will the taste and texture of the pork chop blow your guests away, they'll be awestruck when they see you dunking their dinner in liquid nitrogen.

DUCK CONFIT

There is no more efficient way to confit proteins than by cooking them sous vide, which allows you to carefully control the cooking process and requires much less fat than traditional methods. The resulting flavors are highly concentrated and luxuriously decadent.

Ingredients:

2 each / 0.62 lb. / 283 grams duck legs (566 grams total)
3 teaspoons / 11 grams kosher salt
1/2 teaspoon / 2 grams orange zest
1/8 teaspoon / 0.2 grams ground clove
1/8 teaspoon / 0.2 grams ground black pepper
1 each garlic clove, minced
1 each bay leaf, crumbled
1 each thyme sprig, stripped of its leaves
1/3 cup / 120 grams spiced duck fat (see recipe on page 82)
rice bran or grape seed oil
saffron Israeli couscous (see page 89)

Input data for Sous Vide Toolbox™

Units:	in / mm °F / °C
Protein:	Poultry
Shape:	Whole Thigh / Leg
Cooking Method:	Cook and Pasteurize to Core
Thickness:	1 1/4 inch / 31 mm
Desired Core Temperature:	180°F / 82.2°C
Initial Temperature:	41°F / 5°C
Water Temperature:	180°F / 82.2°C
Ice Bath:	On
Ice Bath Temperature:	33.8°F / 1°C
Final Food Temperature:	41°F / 5°C
Serves:	2

Calculated Times:

Cook Time:	8 hours, 3 minutes
Tenderness Time:	5 hours, 45 minutes
Cooling Time:	1 hour, 8 minutes
Total Time:	9 hours, 11 minutes
	plus 24 hours cure time

Method:

1. Combine the kosher salt, orange zest, clove, black pepper, garlic, bay leaf, and thyme together and coat the duck legs completely in the mixture.

2. Vacuum-seal the duck legs in one even layer with the salt mixture and refrigerate them for 24 hours to cure.

3. Remove the duck legs from the vacuum pouch and rinse off all the salt mixture under cold running water. Pat the legs completely dry with paper towels.

4. Preheat a water bath to 180°F / 82.2°C

5. Place the cured duck legs in a new vacuum pouch with the duck fat, making sure to keep the duck in one layer and vacuum-seal it.

6. Place the duck leg pouch into the water bath and cook it for eight hours.

7. Carefully remove the duck pouch from the water bath and place it in a heavily iced bath for at least 1 hour and 8 minutes.

8. At this time, the duck legs are ready to sear and serve. To sear the duck legs, preheat your oven to 400°F / 204.4°C. Heat an oven-safe non-stick pan over medium-high heat. When you feel strong heat radiating from the pan, add a thin film of oil. When the oil begins to shimmer or look watery, carefully place the duck legs in the pan, skin-side down. Once you begin to see a dark-brown color form around the bottom of the legs, place the pan in the oven and allow the legs to rewarm.

9. The duck legs are ready to serve once they have been warmed through.

Alternatively, you may add a couple of extra steps to the process if you would like to further impress your guests. After step six, remove the duck legs from the vacuum pouch. Hold the duck firmly in one hand and carefully twist out the thigh and leg bones. Place the de-boned legs between two flat trays lined with parchment paper. Gently weigh the top pan down with a half gallon of milk or an item of equivalent weight to "press" the duck into a flat shape. Place the weighted pan combination in the refrigerator overnight to press the skin side of the duck legs perfectly flat, allowing for an even sear. The pressed legs can also be carefully cut into smaller portions.

DUCK BREAST

Cooking duck breast can be tricky. You want to keep it on the medium to rare side, but undercooking it just a little too much can result in a tough texture and gamey flavors. Cooking sous vide eliminates these potential stumbling blocks.

Ingredients:

1 each 8 ounce / 226 grams duck breast

1 tablespoon / 15 grams unsalted butter

1 each thyme sprig

rice bran, grape seed or other neutral-flavored oil with a high smoke point

kosher salt to taste

Input data for Sous Vide Toolbox™

Units:	in / mm °F / °C
Protein:	Poultry
Shape:	Whole boneless breast
Thickness:	1 1/8 inch / 29 mm
Temperature:	135°F / 57.2°C
Cooking Method:	Cook and Pasteurize to Core
Desired Core Temperature:	135°F / 57.2°C
Initial Temperature:	41°F / 5°C
Water Temperature:	135°F / 57.2°C
Serves:	1

Calculated Times:

Cook Time: 2 hours, 54 minutes

Method:

1. Preheat a water bath to 135°F / 57.2°C.

2. Taking care not to cut into the meat, score the duck skin in a cross hatch pattern. (The cuts need only to break the skin.) This will help render fat out from the breast during cooking and searing. It will also help the breast to maintain its shape as it cooks.

3. Place the duck breast, butter and thyme in a vacuum pouch and vacuum-seal it.

4. Place the vacuum pouch in the water bath and cook the duck breast for 2 hours and 54 minutes to pasteurize it to the core.

5. Once the duck breast has reached an internal temperature of at least 135°F / 57.2°C, and desired time has elapsed, remove the vacuum pouch from the water bath and dry the duck breast completely with paper towels. Season the duck breast with kosher salt.

6. To sear the duck breast, preheat a pan over medium-high heat. When you feel strong heat radiating from the pan, add a thin film of oil. When the oil begins to shimmer or look watery, carefully place the duck breast skin-side down in the pan while tilting the pan away from you to avoid the splatter of hot oil. Once you begin to see a dark-brown color form around the bottom of the breast and the skin has crisped to your liking, flip the breast over and cook the underside for 30 seconds.

7. Remove the duck from the pan and allow it to rest for a moment before slicing and serving.

SAFFRON ISRAELI COUSCOUS WITH RAISINS AND EDAMAME

Sous vide cooking lends its benefits to an amazingly wide variety of foods. However, we recognize that other techniques are also vital to creating complete meals. Here's an example of a great recipe that can be easily prepared on the stovetop as a side dish that marries well with many of our suggested sous vide entrées. Alternatively, you might want to occasionally prepare this recipe as a main course.

Parameters:

Cook Time: 10 minutes

Serves: 1 to 2

Ingredients:

1 cup / 133 grams Israeli couscous

1 1/4 cups / 300 grams water

1/3 cup / 51 grams raisins

7 each saffron threads

1 tablespoon / 11 grams olive oil

1 1/2 tablespoons / 3 grams parsley, chopped

1/3 cup / 48 grams edamame, shelled

lemon zest, kosher salt, and cracked black pepper to taste

Method:

1. Combine the couscous, water, raisins and saffron in a pot on the stove. Bring the mixture to a boil.

2. Continue to boil the mixture for 8 minutes. When half of the liquid has been absorbed, add the edamame to the pot to warm the beans through.

3. When all of the liquid has been absorbed and the couscous is tender, add the parsley, lemon zest, kosher salt, black pepper and olive oil to the pot. Toss and serve.

DAVE'S BUTTERMILK FRIED CHICKEN

PolyScience® chef David Pietranczyk helped pick and develop all of our recipes, but he's especially proud of this one. The sous vide method ensures the chicken is crispy yet moist. There's no more need to cut into the pieces to check for doneness. You'll know when they're ready, and they'll remain perfect. Just pull them out of the bath and bread and fry them for a couple of minutes. The reduced frying time also makes the process easier and the outcome a little healthier.

Parameters:

Cook Time:

Breasts:	1 hour, 50 minutes
Thighs and Legs:	3 hours, 3 minutes
	allow 24 hours to brine
Temperature:	149°F / 65°C
Serves:	4

Ingredients:

1 gallon / 3,780 grams water
1/2 cup / 82 grams kosher salt
2 chicken breasts—170 grams each
2 chicken thighs—142 grams each
5 tablespoons / 75 grams unsalted butter
10 each thyme sprigs
2 cups / 477 grams buttermilk
1 each / 62 grams whole egg
2 cups / 308 grams all-purpose flour
2 tablespoons / 10 grams garlic powder
2 tablespoons / 18 grams paprika
1 tablespoon / 10 grams onion flake
1 tablespoon / 13 grams kosher salt
Rice bran oil or your favorite frying oil
kosher salt to taste

Method:

1. Combine the water and salt. (An immersion or stand blender is helpful.) Once all of the salt has dissolved, add the chicken pieces and water-salt blend to a food-safe container and brine for 24 hours.

2. Preheat the water bath to 149°F / 65°C.

3. Remove the chicken pieces from the brine and dry them well with paper towels. (This may take several attempts.)

4. Pair the legs, thighs, and wings in three separate vacuum pouches and vacuum-seal them. Place each breast in its own pouch. Add 1 tablespoon / 15 grams of unsalted butter and 2 thyme sprigs to each pouch, vacuum-seal and refrigerate them.

5. Place the thigh and leg pouches in the water bath and cook for 1 hour and 13 minutes. At this time, add the chicken breasts to the bath and continue to cook for another hour and 50 minutes.

6. Whisk the buttermilk and egg together in a bowl.

7. In another bowl, combine the all-purpose flour, garlic powder and paprika. Whisk the dry ingredients to fully combine them.

8. Preheat a fryer filled with rice bran or your favorite frying oil to 375°F / 190.5°C.

9. After 3 hours and 3 minutes has elapsed, carefully remove the vacuum pouches from the water bath and cut them open. Wrap the chicken pieces in paper towels to dry them completely.

10. Working in batches, dip the chicken pieces in the seasoned flour and shake off the excess, placing the dipped pieces in the buttermilk mixture.

11. Shake off the excess buttermilk from the chicken and place the pieces back into the seasoned flour.

12. Place the chicken in the deep fryer until golden brown.

13. Place the fried chicken pieces onto paper towels to drain off any oil and season lightly with salt. Serve.

Birds have developed hollow, lightweight bones to aid in flight. These bones are very porous and fragile; for this reason they are not ideally suited for use with high-pressure vacuum sealers, and so we recommend using low-vacuum levels when packing poultry.

HERB-INFUSED HONEY

Honey can bring an appealing touch of sweetness to many foods. Placing packaged honey in a sous vide bath is a convenient way to keep it warm and flowing. Adding herbs to the pouch captures their delicate flavors and aromas.

Parameters:

Cook Time:	30 minutes
Temperature:	149°F / 65°C
Yield:	3/4 cup / 158 grams

Ingredients:

3/4 cup / 158 grams honey
1 tablespoon / 4 grams herbs de Provence

Method:

1. Preheat a water bath to 149°F / 65°C.

2. Combine all of the ingredients in a vacuum pouch and vacuum-seal it.

3. Place the vacuum pouch into the water bath and cook for at least 30 minutes to infuse the contents.

4. The infused honey may be kept warm for serving or cooled.

CHATEAUBRIAND FOR TWO

For many people, Chateaubriand is the most sumptuous cut of meat imaginable. Just the name summons up images of elegance and refinement. Another thing we can all agree upon is that it is a cut of meat that is too expensive to cook improperly. Sous vide cooking eliminates all the risk and makes it the best it can be.

Ingredients:

1 Chateaubriand, 1 1/4 pounds / 567 grams
8 tablespoons / 112 grams unsalted butter, divided
2 shallots / 51 grams
3 garlic cloves / 18 grams
8 thyme sprigs, divided
rice bran or grape seed oil or other neutral-flavored oil with a high smoke point
kosher salt to taste

Input data for Sous Vide Toolbox™

Units:	in / mm °F / °C
Protein:	Beef
Shape:	Cylinder
Thickness (diameter):	2 3/4 inch / 70 mm
Temperature:	137°F/ 58.3°C
Yield:	2 Steaks
Cooking Method:	Cook and Pasteurize to Surface
Desired Core Temperature:	137°F / 58.3°C
Initial Temperature:	41°F / 5°C
Water Temperature:	137°F / 58.3°C
Serves:	2

Cooking time to temperature (Slow Method)

Water Temperature:	137°F / 58.3°C

Cooking time to temperature (Fast Method)

Water Temperature:	138°F / 58.9°C

Calculated Times:
Slow Method: 4 hours, 28 minutes
Fast Method: 2 hours, 58 minutes

Method:

1. Preheat a water bath to 137°F / 58.3°C.

2. Place half of the butter, half of the thyme, beef and shallots in a vacuum pouch and vacuum-seal it.

3. Once the bath has reached temperature, place the vacuum pouch in the bath and cook for 4 hours and 28 minutes.

4. When the beef has reached your desired core temperature, remove the beef from the vacuum pouch and dry the surface completely with paper towels.

5. Heat a sauté pan over high heat. When you feel strong heat radiating from the pan, add a thin film of oil. When the oil begins to shimmer or look watery, carefully lay the beef in the pan while tilting the pan away from you to avoid the splatter of hot oil.

6. Once you begin to see a dark-brown color form around the bottom of the beef and it has released itself from the pan, roll it to sear another side. Repeat until seared on all sides.

7. Add the garlic and remaining half of the butter and thyme to the pan. Baste the beef with the hot foamy butter. Once the butter begins to turn deep brown, remove the beef from the pan and allow it to rest for 1 minute before slicing.

We've said it before, but it's important enough to say it again. Increasing the thickness of the meat being cooked will increase cooking times exponentially. Doubling the thickness, for example, will more than double the cook time, so plan accordingly.

Many chefs insert a hypodermic thermocouple type probe into the food while in the pouch to determine the exact core temperature. When doing so, make sure that the tip of the probe is at the very center of the thickest part of whatever you are cooking. Once the food has reached your desired temperature, pull the pouch out of the bath to ensure that it does not continue to cook. Alternatively, lower the bath temperature to your desired core temperature.

This recipe contribution from Bruno Goussault, an early sous vide pioneer and chief scientist at the Culinary Research and Education Academy (see pages 30-31), is about much more than simply making a wonderful rack of lamb with artichokes. It illustrates a fundamental difference in the way many European chefs utilize sous vide. They tend to begin the cooking process at higher temperatures and then reduce those temperatures in order to re-create the textures achieved by traditional cooking methods. By starting the bath at a higher temperature, the outer portion will be more done and have a more firm texture. By reducing the temperature later in the process, the center can gently be warmed and tenderized, producing the kind of results that are hallmarks of the sous vide process.

The recipe as it appears on the following page was written by Bruno in his own style.

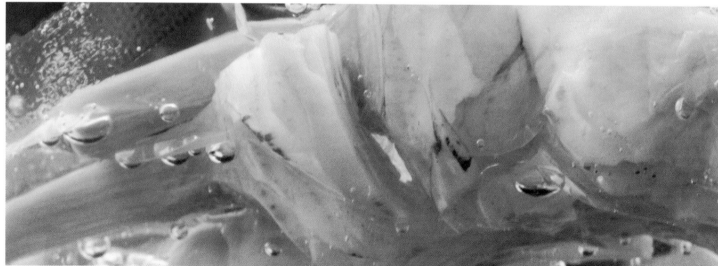

Ingredients (serves two)

Rack of Lamb		Lamb juice		Artichoke	
800 grams	1 rack of lamb	1/2	yellow onion	1.2 kilograms	artichoke (3 pieces)
4 grams	thyme	1	carrot	6 grams	salt
5 cc	canola oil	1	*bouquet garni*	2	lemons
8 grams	salt				
0.8 grams	pepper				

---

method

---

1. **Preparation :**

   Rack of lamb

   Cut out and remove the top of rack (skin, fat and cartilage)

   Clean bones on rack

   Debone the backbone (la chainette)

   Heat oil in a pan to color the rack on each side (3x30 seconds) for each side

   Store in blast chiller until core temperature is below 40°F/6°C

   Lamb juice

   Color bones, skin, small pieces of lamb and fat in pan with canola oil

   Add carrots, onion in small cubes and *bouquet garni,*

   After 5 minutes add cold water and boil slowly for one and a half hours, control the seasoning, pass through the China cap sieve.

   Melt in pan 20 grams of butter and when it is colored add the lamb juice, put in blast chiller.

2. **Cooking & Chilling :**

   Rack of lamb

   1st step 181 °F/83°C for 4 minutes

   2nd step 151°F/66°C ambient to 95°F/35°C

   3rd step 140°F/60°C ambient to 113°F/45 °C

   4th step 131°F/55°C ambient to 131°F/55°C

   Then step-by-step chilling; 10 minutes in air of kitchen, 10 minutes in room temperature water and 2 hours in iced water.

   Lamb juice

   Is pasteurized at 181 °F/83°C for 20 minutes

   Chilling directly in iced water

   Artichoke

   181 °F/83°C for 200 minutes

   Chill directly in iced water

   Preservation minimum 2 weeks in cooler at 32°F/0°C

3. **Packing:**

   When each element of recipe is cold, season with salt 0.8% and pepper 0.1% and aromatic herbs and introduce in bags to pack sous vide with adapted program. For artichoke add 1% of grape seed oil to fix the aroma of artichoke. Don't forget to protect bones with aluminum foil.

   Rack of lamb: residual pressure 20 mbar and 15 sec. for additional time.

   Lamb Juice: residual pressure 20 mbar and 0 sec.

   Artichoke: residual pressure 20 mbar and 60 sec. for additional time.

4. **Reheating :**

   Rack of lamb

   15 minutes in circulator at 131°F/56° then open the bag and sear again in salamander or other type of broiler.

   Artichoke and lamb juice

   15 minutes in circulator at 151°F/66°C.

   Presentation :

5. On plate, cut the rack of lamb following bones, slice artichokes and put on plate, artichoke on bottom, sliced artichoke on top and sauce around.

DESSERT

I have had the honor of calling Philip Preston, a.k.a. P Squared (my nickname for him), a friend since the day we met. He's truly one of the most intelligent, humble and generous people I have ever been acquainted with. Over my decade tenure at the 4 star New York Times *and 3 Michelin star-rated restaurant Jean Georges, I spent a lot of time brainstorming and collaborating with Philip on new ideas and uses for his equipment in my pastry kitchen. His products allowed me to set our desserts far apart from many in the world. I have always been — and always will be — a huge fan of the man and the PolyScience brand.*

Johnny Iuzzini

Renowned pastry chef, and author of *Dessert FourPlay:
Sweet Quartets from a Four-Star Pastry Chef* and *Sugar Rush*

COCONUT ICE CREAM

Recipe courtesy of Johnny Iuzzini

Chef Johnny Iuzzini is an award-winning pastry chef and a great friend of mine. He honed his craft at highly influential restaurants including The River Café, Daniel, Payard, Café Boulud and Jean Georges. In 2006, the James Beard Foundation awarded him the "Pastry Chef of the Year." He has been recognized as one of the "10 Most Influential Pastry Chefs in America" by Forbes, "Best New Pastry Chef" by New York Magazine, and named one of the "Top Ten Pastry Chefs in America" two years in a row by Pastry Art & Design. His books include Dessert Fourplay and Sugar Rush. So I am especially proud to showcase this dessert that he created especially for us.

Ingredients:

1520 grams milk
800 grams cream
180 grams milk powder
100 grams trimoline
80 grams atomized glucose
360 grams sugar
8 grams stabilizer
900 grams coconut puree

Special Equipment:

burr mixer

Method:

1. Combine milk, cream, glucose powder, milk powder and trimoline and bring to a simmer.

2. Add sugar that has been mixed well with the stabilizer.

3. Bring to a boil, burr mix and cool.

4. Add in the coconut puree, burr mix again and spin immediately.

5. Freeze metal demi-sphere shells in the freezer.

6. Using a spoon, quickly spread a ½-inch-thick shell of coconut sorbet into the frozen metal demi-sphere shells and refreeze.

7. Once very frozen, dip the metal shells into warm water, remove the coconut ice cream shell.

8. Return to the freezer.

AERATED COCONUT PASSION CURD

Recipe courtesy of Johnny Iuzzini

I developed this recipe for a 2013 episode of Iron Chef America I competed in. In fact, it was the first-ever dessert-only battle. I knew I had to get a lot done in 60 minutes, so I was looking for a way to save time and still cook with precision, and that's where Philip Preston came in. I vacuum-sealed and cooked my passion fruit curd in a PolyScience® immersion circulator. This saved me invaluable time and allowed me to keep my hands free for other tasks. The curd came out perfect, which was integral to me securing a win on the show.

Ingredients:
250 grams passion purée
250 grams eggs
250 grams butter
150 grams sugar
2 leaves gelatin, bloomed
toasted coconut

Special Equipment:
1-liter whipping siphon, 2 nitrous oxide charges
metal demi-sphere shells

Method:

1. Combine all ingredients, blend in blender.

2. Cryovac and cook in a pre-heated water bath at 185°F/ 85°C.

3. Blend, strain, add bloomed gelatin, blend well.

4. Fill whipping siphon, chill partially and charge with 1 N_2O.

5. Shake well and chill.

To Assemble:

6. When ready to serve, have a bowl of hot melted bitter chocolate ready.

7. Have unsweetened shredded coconut toasted, cooled and on a sheet tray.

8. Remove the 2 half spheres of ice cream from the freezer.

9. Working very quickly, add two tablespoons of fresh passion fruit seeds to the bottom of the coconut shell and add aerated curd to fill 3/4 of the way to the top of other shell. Close two halves of top together.

10. Pour chocolate onto a tray, quickly and carefully roll in the melted chocolate.

11. Roll in toasted coconut. Serve.

I usually use liquid nitrogen throughout the process but eliminated it for home cooks.

BANANA CREAM PIE

Banana cream pie is a dinner classic that everyone loves. Sous vide makes preparing it easy and foolproof, so don't be intimidated. Sous vide makes the eggs silkier and the bananas sweeter, creating a banana cream pie that has no equal.

Parameters:

Cook Time: 2 hours
Temperature: 149°F / 65°C - 167°F / 75°C
Yield: 1 9-inch pie

Ingredients:

4 each / 48 grams egg yolks, broken up
3 each / 536 grams bananas, whole, not peeled
4 1/3 each / 11 grams silver leaf gelatin
1 each 13.5 oz. / 403 grams can coconut milk
1/2 cup / 103 grams sugar
3/4 cup / 185 grams whole milk
1 teaspoon / 4 grams kosher salt
sweetened, whipped cream, as needed
toasted coconut (page 102), as needed

Method:

1. Preheat a water bath to 149°F / 65°C.
2. Vacuum-seal the egg yolks and cook them for 15 minutes.
3. Remove them from the water bath and place them into a heavily iced bath. Increase the bath temperature to 167°F / 75°C.
4. Vacuum-seal the bananas and cook them for 2 hours.
5. Remove them from the water bath and place them into a heavily iced bath.
6. Place the gelatin in a bowl of heavily iced water and allow it to bloom.
7. Combine the coconut milk, sugar, whole milk, and salt in a pot on the stove over medium-high heat. Bring the mixture to a boil and add the bloomed gelatin.
8. Once the gelatin has fully dissolved, remove the pot from heat and cool it to room temperature.
9. In a blender, combine the bananas, cooked yolks and coconut milk mixture. Blend the mixture until completely smooth.
10. Chill the mixture to room temperature.
11. Pour the banana mixture into a prepared pie crust (see our version below) and allow it to set overnight in the refrigerator.
12. To serve, top the pie with sweetened whipped cream and toasted coconut.

PIE CRUST

This recipe is my favorite recipe for a classic all-butter crust. Just cut back on the sugar to 1 teaspoon for savory applications.

Parameters:

Cook Time: 1 hour, 30 minutes
Yield: 1 9-inch pie

Ingredients:

1 1/4 cup / 180 grams all-purpose flour
2 teaspoons / 9 grams sugar
1/2 teaspoon / 1.5 grams kosher salt
8 tablespoons / 113 grams unsalted butter
ice water, as needed
flour, as needed
32 ounces of dried beans, for blind baking

Method:

1. Preheat an oven to 425°F / 220°C.
2. Carefully grate the butter on a box grater and place the shredded butter in the freezer for 30 minutes.
3. Once the butter has frozen, combine the flour, sugar, salt and butter in a food processor. Pulse the mixture a few times until the mixture is crumbly in texture.
4. Slowly drizzle the water in, a tablespoon at a time, pulsing the mixture as you pour. The dough should clump together when squeezed.
5. Turn the dough out from the food processor and shape it into a flat disk. Refrigerate it for 30 minutes to rest.
6. Roll the out on a lightly floured work surface and insert the dough into a pie pan. Trim the dough as needed and crimp the edges. Return the dough to the refrigerator for 30 minutes
7. Remove the pie crust from the refrigerator. Prick the bottom of the pie crust generously with a fork.
8. Line the inside of the pie crust with parchment paper and fill the lined crust with the dried beans.
9. Blind bake the pie crust for 10 minutes.
10. Remove the beans and parchment paper from the pie crust. Continue to bake the pie crust until golden brown and fully crisp.
11. Allow the pie crust to cool fully before using.

TOASTED COCONUT

We've found that most toasted coconut you find in stores is overly sweet with an unpleasant "papery" consistency. By contrast, this recipe produces great textures and deep complex flavors.

Parameters:

Cook Time: 30 minutes
Yield: 2 cups

Ingredients:

1 each / whole coconut

Method:

1. Preheat an oven to 375°F / 190°C
2. Drill a hole through 2 of the 3 circular soft spots on the coconut and shake the coconut empty of its water.
3. Place the coconut in the oven for 15-20 minutes until it begins to crack.
4. Split the coconut gently with a hammer along the cracks.
5. Carefully wedge a spoon between the coconut meat and the shell. Pry the coconut away in large pieces. Be aware, the shell is extremely sharp.
6. Using a peeler, peel the coconut meat of the brown papery coating.
7. Shave the cleaned coconut meat pieces on a mandolin as thinly as possible.
8. Spread the coconut shavings on a sheet tray lined with parchment paper and place it back in the oven.
9. Bake the coconut for approximately 10 minutes until the coconut is crispy and begins to brown. Take care to stir the coconut halfway through baking. Reserve the coconut crisps.

MALTED CARAMEL SAUCE

While this recipe is not cooked sous vide, it is a great way to demonstrate one of the many other benefits of a sous vide water bath – the ability to keep side dishes or sauces warm without over-reducing or scorching. We picked this sauce because it's a great addition to our vanilla bean ice cream.

Parameters:
Temperature: 165°F / 73.9°C
Yield: 3 cups

Ingredients:
1 1/2 cups / 300 grams granulated sugar
1 tablespoon / 18 grams light corn syrup or glucose
1/2 cup / 100 grams water
1 1/4 cups / 300 grams heavy whipping cream, scalded
1/2 tablespoon / 6 grams kosher salt
2 tablespoons / 13 grams malted milk powder

1. Combine the water and sugar in a small saucepan.

2. Bring the sugar and water mixture to a boil. Continue to cook without stirring until a candy thermometer reads 350°F / 176.7°C.

3. Remove the candy thermometer from the pot and carefully add the cream, pouring away from you. The sauce will begin to bubble furiously and the caramel will seize.

4. Add the salt and malted milk powder to the pot. Return the mixture to a boil, whisking constantly.

5. Once all of the hard caramel has been dissolved in the cream, transfer the caramel sauce to a container and either chill the mixture down completely or keep it warm in a sous vide bath set to 165°F / 73.9°C.

Many recipes, whether they are cooked traditionally or sous vide, may be held at a constant temperature for service in a water bath. Mashed potatoes for example are incredibly hard to keep warm without drying them out or scorching them. You can either place them in a zip-top bag, and clip the top over the side of the water bath or vacuum seal them and hold them in a 165°F / 73.9°C bath to keep them warm without any fear of burning the bottom of the pot.

SPICE POACHED APPLES

Marinating Granny Smith apples in cider vinegar may seem like a simple and subtle choice, but the results can be quite dramatic. This recipe delivers a classic acidic-sweet burst of flavor and a wonderfully crispy yet tender texture.

Parameters:

Thickness:	1 1/4 inch / 32 mm
Cook Time:	45 minutes
Temperature:	183.2°F / 84°C
Serves:	3 to 4

Ingredients:
3 each / 420 grams Granny Smith apples, peeled, cored and quartered
1 3/4 cups / 355 grams granulated sugar
3 ounces / 86 grams water
3 ounces / 86 grams cider vinegar
1/2 teaspoon / 1 gram ground green cardamom
1 tablespoon / 6 grams ground cinnamon
1 tablespoon / 14 grams vanilla bean paste
1/4 teaspoon / 1 gram kosher salt

Method:

1. Preheat a water bath to 183.2°F / 84°C

2. Combine the sugar, water, cider vinegar, cardamom, cinnamon, vanilla bean paste, and salt in a pot and bring them to a boil over high heat. Once the mixture has come to a boil, turn it off and allow to chill to room temperature.

3. Remove the mixture from the pot and cool to at least 41°F / 5°C.

4. Place 1/3 cup / 103 grams of the chilled syrup and apples in a vacuum pouch, keeping the apples in a single layer. Vacuum-seal the apples and syrup. Reserve the rest of the syrup for another use.

5. Place the vacuum pouch into the water bath and warm them for 45 minutes.

6. Remove the apples from the water bath and carefully cut the bag open.

7. Slice the apple quarters into three wedges while they are still warm and serve.

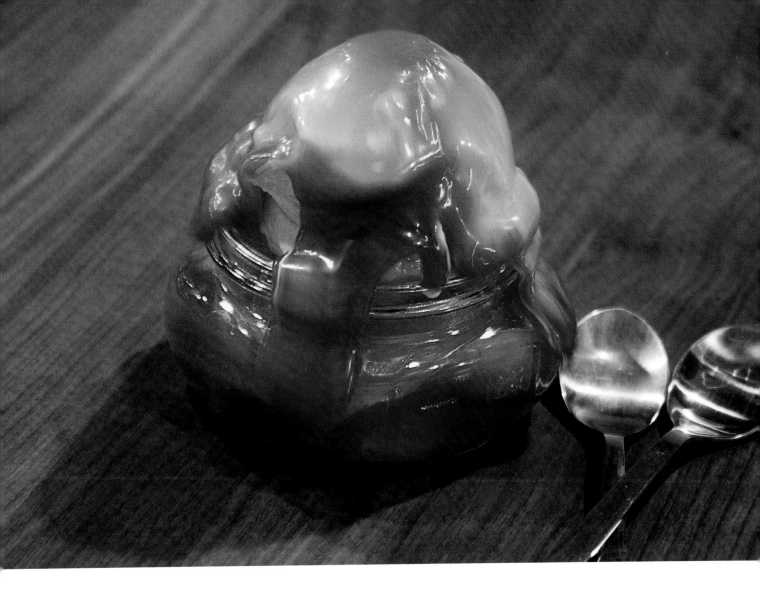

VANILLA BEAN ICE CREAM

One of the challenges of making an egg-based ice cream base is the need to delicately cook the mixture in order to pasteurize the raw eggs. Cooking the mixture over a stovetop can be challenging to get it just right. That exact temperature is easy to achieve with sous vide cooking by simply setting the desired bath temperature, making it easy to create restaurant-worthy ice cream. You might also look toward sous vide cooking to make your own ice cream toppings.

Parameters:

Cook Time: 45 minutes
Temperature: 181°F / 82.7°C
Serves: 3

Ingredients:

6 each / 100 grams egg yolks
1 cup / 238 grams 2% milk
1 cup / 253 grams heavy whipping cream
3/8 cup / 85 grams sugar
1 tablespoon / 14 grams vanilla bean paste
1/2 teaspoon / 2 grams kosher salt

Method:

1.   Prepare a water bath heated to 181°F / 82.7°C.

2.   Place all ingredients in a blender and blend on low until smooth.

3.   Place the ice cream mixture into a vacuum pouch and vacuum-seal.

4.   Place the vacuum pouch into the water bath and cook sous vide for 45 minutes.

5.   Remove the ice cream base from the water bath and submerge the pouch in a heavily iced bath until it has cooled completely.

6.   Pour the contents of the bag into a blender and blend until the mixture is completely smooth.

7.   Pass the blended mixture through a fine-mesh sieve and freeze according to the time outlined by your ice cream maker's instruction manual. Reserve in the freezer until ready to serve.

CLASSIC POUNDCAKE

This classic pound cake recipe doesn't involve sous vide, but it's a great base for toppings, sauces and sweets that can be prepared with an immersion circulator. For example, just spoon on bourbon-infused peaches (page 43), blueberry compote (page 45) or the crème anglaise from the vanilla bean ice cream (page 103) recipe instead of freezing it. These combinations transform a familiar comfort-food classic into a decadent revelation.

Parameters:

Cook Time: 1 hour
Yield: 1 poundcake

Ingredients:

2 sticks / 226 grams unsalted butter, softened
8 ounces (by weight) / 226 grams granulated sugar
4.5 each / 261 grams whole eggs
1 tablespoon / 14 grams vanilla bean paste
1 teaspoon / 1 gram kosher salt
8 ounces (by weight) / 226 grams cake flour

Method:

1. Preheat the oven to 350°F / 176.6°C.

2. Spray the inside of a 9-by-5-inch loaf pan with non-stick baking spray and dust the inside with a thin layer of cake flour.

3. Combine the butter and sugar in a stand mixer fitted with a paddle attachment. Cream the butter and sugar on medium until the butter is light and airy.

4. Scrape down the sides of the bowl. Add the eggs, one at a time, waiting until each egg is fully incorporated before adding the next. Once all of the eggs are incorporated into the batter, add the vanilla bean paste and salt. Increase the speed to medium until the mixture looks silky and smooth.

5. Stop the machine again and scrape down the sides of the bowl. Turn the machine to its lowest setting and add the flour in three separate pours, scraping down the sides of the bowl between each. Take care not to overwork the batter.

6. Pour the batter into the prepared loaf pan and bake at 350°F / 176.6°C for approximately 1 hour or until an instant read thermometer placed in the center of the cake indicates 210°F / 98.9°C.

7. Allow the pan to cool on a resting rack for a few minutes before turning the cake out. Allow the cake to cool completely before slicing.

LEMON CURD

Cooking lemon curd using traditional equipment such as a double boiler can be tedious and often results in overcooking. Sous vide simplifies the process allowing you to cook all the ingredients together at a constant temperature, ensuring a perfect curd each time.

Parameters:

Cook Time: 1 hour
Temperature: 167°F / 75°C
Yield: 1 3/4 cups

Ingredients:

2 each / 113 grams whole eggs
1/2 cup / 142 grams sugar
1/4 cup / 55 grams lemon juice
11 tablespoons / 155 grams unsalted butter
1 each / 1 gram lemon, zested

Method:

1. Preheat the water bath to 167°F / 75°C.

2. Combine all of the ingredients in a vacuum pouch and vacuum-seal it.

3. Place the vacuum pouch in the water bath and cook for 1 hour.

4. Remove the pouch from the water bath and pour the contents into a blender.

5. Blend the mixture until it is fully emulsified.

6. Pour the lemon curd into a bowl set in heavily iced water. Gently stir the lemon curd, scraping the sides frequently, until the mixture reaches room temperature.

7. Once the lemon curd begins to visibly set and thicken in texture, transfer the bowl to the refrigerator and allow it to fully set.

COCKTAILS

1. Glögg

2. Peach Gin & Tonic

3. Apple-Rosemary Martini

4. Ginger-Citrus Mocktail

5. Manhattan with Sous Vide Bitters

6. The Host

GLÖGG

This is a recipe for traditional Scandinavian mulled wine that gets a boost from the addition of port and aquavit. The result is ideal for seasonal entertaining. The intense flavor, which is perfect for winter holidays, is fully captured with the alcohol after being slow cooked in sealed sous vide packages.

Parameters:

Cook Time: 2 hours
Temperature: 158°F / 70°C
Serves: Six 5 oz. drinks

Ingredients:

2 cups / 394 grams dry red wine
2 cups / 428 grams port
1 cup / 180 grams aquavit
1/2 cup / 104 grams sugar
1/2 each / 200 grams orange, sliced
1/4 cup / 37 grams dark raisins
1/4 cup / 40 grams blanched almonds
2 each / 10 grams cinnamon stick
1/2 teaspoon / 1 gram green cardamom seeds, crushed
5 each / 1 gram whole cloves
1 each / 1 gram whole star anise

Method:

1. Preheat your water bath to 158°F / 70°C.

2. Combine all of the ingredients in a vacuum pouch and vacuum-seal it.

3. Place the pouch into the water bath and cook it for 2 hours.

4. Remove the pouch and place it in a heavily iced bath.

5. Refrigerate the mixture overnight.

6. Open the pouch and strain the contents through a fine-mesh sieve.

7. Reseal the liquid in six different 5-ounce portioned vacuum bags and refrigerate.

8. When ready to serve, place the pouches in a water bath preheated to at least 165°F / 73.9°C for at least 10 minutes.

9. Once the pouch has been rewarmed, pour the contents into a serving glass.

PEACH-INFUSED GIN

Bartenders and mixologists often age spirits with fruit for months to achieve richer and more balanced fruit profiles. In this recipe, the application of gentle heat speeds the process up to just hours, and because all the ingredients are in a sealed bag, there's no loss of flavor or alcohol. Try some different fruit and spirits combinations.

Parameters:

Cook time: 2 hours
Temperature: 158°F / 70°C
Yield: 2 cups

Ingredients:

5 each / 563 grams peaches, cut into wedges
2 cups / 400 grams gin

Method:

1. Preheat the water bath to 158°F / 70°C.

2. Combine the peaches and gin in a vacuum pouch.

3. Vacuum-seal the pouch and cook for 2 hours.

4. Remove the pouch from the water and place it in a heavily iced bath.

5. Refrigerate the infused gin overnight.

PEACH GIN AND TONIC

Gin is a great medium for fruit flavors. I'm sure you'll agree after the first sip of this easy-to-make riff on a classic gin and tonic.

Ingredients:

2 ounces / 50 grams peach-infused gin
3/4 ounce / 20 grams tonic syrup
4 ounces / 100 grams soda water
1 each lime wedge

Method:

1. Combine the gin and tonic syrup in a mixing glass and stir.

2. Pour the tonic mixture into a glass filled with ice.

3. Top the tonic mixture with soda water.

4. Garnish the drink with a lime wedge.

GRAPEFRUIT FOAM

A little grapefruit foam can go a long way toward sprucing up simple cocktails, including a classic margarita, but it also can be used in conjunction with some savory preparations as well. Set atop a light salad or laced onto a plank of salmon, this versatile foam can add a shock of citrus and just the right hint of astringency.

Parameters:
Yield: 3 cups

Ingredients:
3 cup / 810 grams grapefruit juice
4 tablespoon / 46 grams simple syrup
5-1/3 each / 12.8 grams silver leaf gelatin

Special Equipment:
1-liter whipping siphon, 2 nitrous oxide charges

Method:

1. Bloom the gelatin in 1 cup / 327 grams of the grapefruit juice.

2. Once the gelatin has fully softened, heat the grapefruit-gelatin mixture over gentle heat until the gelatin has fully dissolved.

3. Blend the remaining grapefruit juice, simple syrup and gelatin mixture until well mixed.

4. Place the gelatin mixture in the refrigerator to fully set.

5. Once set, fill a 1-liter whipping siphon with the gelatin mixture to the manufacturer's marked fill line.

6. Charge the whipping siphon with 2 nitrous oxide charges, shaking vigorously after each charge. Reserve.

GINGER-CITRUS MOCKTAIL

This recipe requires you to make ginger syrup. It's easy to master, and the technique can be used to make any other flavor that comes to mind. You can also use the carbonation technique to make other types of soda as well.

Special Equipment:

1-liter whipping siphon, 2 carbon dioxide charges (CO_2)

Ingredients:

1 1/2 cups ginger soda base
grapefruit foam (see page 110)
1 each mint sprig

Method:

1. Pour the soda base into a whipping siphon and charge it with 2 carbon dioxide charges.

2. Fill a glass with ice and dispense the soda base into the glass, filling it 3/4 full.

3. Top the soda with the grapefruit foam, filling the remaining 1/4 of the glass.

4. Garnish the drink with a mint sprig.

GINGER-LIME SODA BASE

This refreshingly spicy-sweet riff on a ginger beer soda fizzes together deeply concentrated citrus and ginger notes to create a truly effervescent summertime sipper. Children can enjoy it straight up, while cocktail-lovers can use it as a base for some creative warm-weather tipples.

Parameters:

Cook Time:	1 hour
Temperature:	140°F / 60°C
Yield:	1 1/2 cups

Ingredients:

3/4 cup / 156 grams sugar
3/4 cup / 170 grams water
1 8-inch / 188 grams knob of ginger, thinly sliced
1/2 cup / 120 grams lime juice

Method:

1. Place your immersion circulator on your desired cooking vessel and preheat your water bath to 140°F / 60°C.

2. Combine the sugar, water and ginger in a vacuum pouch and vacuum-seal.

3. Place the vacuum pouch in the water bath and cook for 1 hour.

4. Place the pouch in a heavily iced bath. Once chilled, the syrup is ready to use.

5. Combine the ginger syrup with the lime juice. Reserve.

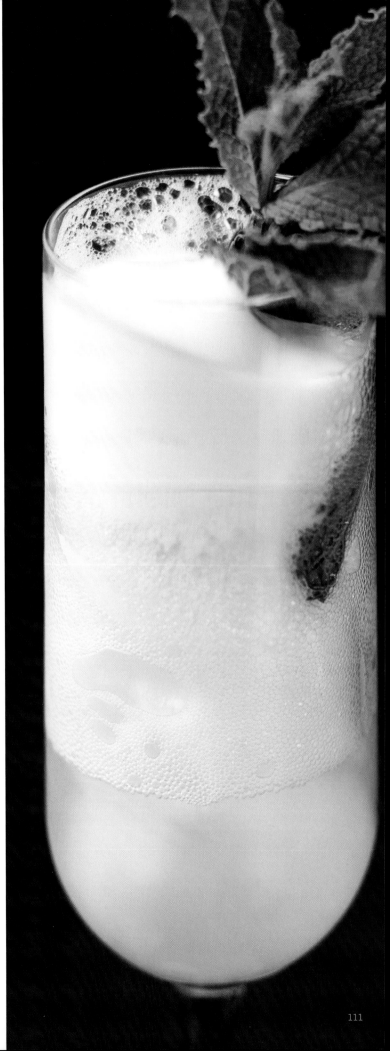

MANHATTAN WITH SOUS VIDE BITTERS

The Manhattan is such a classic cocktail — the perfect blend of bourbon, sweet cherries and botanical bitters — that it's difficult to change a single note of flavor, but by improving the quality of the bitters, you can add an extra touch of class to an already elegant drink.

Ingredients:
2 1/2 ounces / 52 grams bourbon whiskey
3/4 ounce / 17 grams red vermouth
2 dashes PSC Bitters Batch 01
2 each cherries
1 each orange zest strip

Method:

1. Fill a mixing glass with ice.

2. Add the bourbon and the vermouth to the mixing glass.

3. Add two cherries to the cocktail glass.

4. Stir the Manhattan until well chilled and pour it over the cherries.

5. Rim the cocktail with the orange zest and twist it over the drink.

6. Add 2 dashes of bitters to the cocktail.

PSC BITTERS BATCH 01

This recipe is a great introductory recipe for making your own bitters. And while you will find yourself using these bitters in cocktails, try sprinkling them atop ice cream for a truly unique topping; you'll be amazed how well these earthy flavors meld with the sweet creamy ice cream. The name "PSC" is derived as an abbreviation for PolyScience® Culinary, as this is considered our house recipe.

Parameters:
Cook Time: 1 hour
Temperature: 140°F / 60°C
Yield: 2 cups

Ingredients:
2 cups / 500 grams vodka
1/3 cup + 1 tablespoon / 90 grams packed brown sugar
1/3 cup / 40 grams fresh orange peel
1 each / 3.5 grams vanilla bean, seeded
2 teaspoons / 4 grams gentian root
2 teaspoons / 5 grams wild cherry bark
1 teaspoon / 4.5 grams grains of paradise
1 each / 2 grams tonka bean, grated
1 each / 1 grams whole star anise
11 each / 2 grams whole clove

Method:

1. Preheat your water bath to 140°F / 60°C.

2. Combine all of the ingredients in a vacuum pouch and vacuum-seal it.

3. Cook the pouch for 1 hour and then place the pouch in a heavily iced bath and allow it to cool completely before opening the bag.

4. The bitters will be ready to strain and use immediately, but for best results, refrigerate the pouch overnight.

5. Strain the solids from the bitters using a fine-mesh sieve.

6. Reserve the liquid.

APPLE-INFUSED GIN

Apples and gin are a great combination of flavors; the rich aromatics of the gin contrast well against the bright acidic flavor of the green apple. There is an unlimited variety of ingredients you can use to infuse the gin, and experimentation is encouraged.

Parameters:

Cook Time: 2 hours
Temperature: 122°F / 50°C
Yield: 2 cups

Ingredients:

2 each / 485 grams Granny Smith apples, peeled and shaved into 1/8 inch / 3 mm slices
2 cups / 400 grams gin

Method:

1. Preheat the water bath to 122°F / 50°C.

2. Combine the apples and gin in a vacuum pouch.

3. Vacuum-seal the pouch and cook for 2 hours.

4. Remove the pouch from the water and place it in a heavily iced bath.

5. Refrigerate the infused gin overnight.

6. Strain the infused gin through a fine mesh sieve. Discard the apples.

APPLE-ROSEMARY MARTINI

This recipe is a variation on an old James Bond classic: the martini, shaken not stirred. You'll be surprised how the addition of just a few drops of homemade bitters can make such a big difference.

Ingredients:

2 1/2 ounces / 59 grams apple-infused gin
1/2 ounce / 14 grams dry vermouth
1 each rosemary sprig
2 each apple pieces
2 dashes PSC Bitters Batch 01 (see page 112)

Method:

1. Combine the gin and vermouth in a Boston shaker filled with ice.

2. Place the rosemary in the mixing glass.

3. Shake the mixture over ice.

4. Place the apple pieces in the glass.

5. Pour the martini through a Collins strainer over the apples.

6. Add 2 dashes of PolyScience® Bitters Batch 01 to the cocktail and serve.

THE HOST

This cocktail was coined "The Host" because it helps make entertaining so easy and rewarding. Simply vacuum-seal and gently heat bourbon in individual packages and then pour the contents over your choice of flavorings in a French press coffee maker. The results are outstanding. Experiment with aromatic ingredients such as sage, cinnamon, orange and lemon zest, cinnamon, star anise, black peppercorns, etc.

Parameters:

Cook Time: 14 minutes
Temperature: 185°F / 85°C
Yield: Two 7 oz. drinks

Ingredients:

4 ounces / 100 grams bourbon
10 ounces / 200 grams apple cider
1/2 ounce / 20 grams barrel-aged maple syrup

Method:

1. Preheat a water bath to 185°F / 85°C.

2. Combine the bourbon, apple cider and maple syrup in a vacuum pouch and vacuum-seal it.

3. Place the vacuum pouch in the preheated bath for 10 minutes.

4. Fill a French press with aromatics to your liking.

5. After the bourbon mixture has sufficiently heated through, pour the hot liquid into a French press and allow it to steep for 4 minutes.

6. After 4 minutes has elapsed, press the plunger and serve.

TECHNICAL REFERENCE

SOUS VIDE PACKAGING INSIGHTS

Chris Young

Co-founder of ChefSteps.com & a co-author of *Modernist Cuisine*

Sous vide packaging has a difficult job: These plastic pouches must be both watertight and airtight, and they need to be strong at relatively high cooking temperatures, yet flexible when very cold. Unfortunately, no single plastic has all of these characteristics.

That's why sous vide packages are highly engineered products, composed of two different kinds of plastic, for optimal performance under any condition. The best packaging consists of inner layers of polyethylene (a strong, waterproof plastic), and an outer layer of nylon (an excellent barrier to oxygen, steam and other gases). The result is a clear plastic bag that can meet the needs of a demanding kitchen environment.

But are these plastics safe? Most of us have seen media reports that raise concerns about unhealthy chemicals leaching into food and drink from plastic containers. It's entirely reasonable, then, that people are concerned about the plastics used in sous vide packaging.

At ChefSteps, we've reviewed the scientific literature and found that, according to the most recent research, the polyethylene used as the inner layer of high-quality sous vide packaging is generally considered to be biologically inert. Under realistic sous vide cooking conditions, researchers have not detected potentially unhealthy compounds such as bisphenol-A (BPA), phthalates, or compounds with suspected estrogen activity (EA) in this type of plastic. Both polyethylene and nylon plastics have also passed the Ames test and other studies of potential mutagenic toxicity.

Researchers have shown, however, that under extreme "stressing" conditions, polyethylene can leach chemicals that produce harmful estrogen activity. These conditions include superheating polyethylene, exposing it to UV light, and washing it with pure ethanol, none of which is at all likely to occur during sous vide cooking. Nevertheless, most reputable manufacturers of sous vide packing have now gone further to eliminate even this small risk, using versions of nylon and polyethylene plastics certified as EA-free.

Chris Young and Grant Lee Crilly are co-founders of ChefSteps.com; Chris is also noted as being a co-author of *Modernist Cuisine*

RISK FACTORS IN PREPARING SOUS VIDE FOODS

Whether you are cooking for friends and family in your own home or for a dining room full of customers in a restaurant setting, you are likely to encounter questions about the safety of cooking sous vide. The more you know about the process, the more you can communicate to your guests, so we asked Dr. O. Peter Snyder Jr., one of the foremost authorities on sous vide and food safety, to break down the process on a cellular level. Here are his insights:

Sous vide products are foods such as meat, fish, poultry, fruits and vegetables that have been sealed under vacuum in a low-oxygen-transmission plastic film pouch, and the pouch is immersed in a constant-temperature water bath and cooked for a time that provides adequate reduction of pathogenic vegetative bacteria and a desired tenderization. Meat shrinkage in cooking meat, poultry and fish does not take place significantly until the meat temperature is 130°F/54°C or hotter. Typically, the tougher the meat, the richer and better the flavor — but drier — unless these tougher cuts (briskets, flanks and ribs) are cooked sous vide in a sealed pouch, where all of the juices are retained, and the temperature is low enough so as to not cause muscle shrinkage. The foods cooked in this manner are generally thin, less than two inches thick. Cooking times in a moderate temperature water bath can be a couple of hours in order to get the food center temperature to 130°F/54°C or above. People believe that cooking is for a desired quality. Actually, the primary purpose of cooking is to pasteurize the food to reduce vegetative pathogens to meet a Food-Safety Objective (FSO) that provides an Appropriate Level of Protection (ALOP) to assure safety.

There are no significant chemical or physical hazards associated with sous vide cooking. The question is: What are the biological hazards? There are two classes of pathogens in sous vide meat, fish and poultry products: vegetative pathogens and spore pathogens. Vegetative pathogens are destroyed as a function of time as temperatures reach 130°F/54°C. They are killed slowly at about 130°F/54°C, with a 6.5-log reduction of *Salmonella* (the target organism) at 112 minutes. At 140°F/60°C, *Salmonella* dies 10 times faster, or after 12 minutes. At 158°F/70°C, it is considered to be an instant 6.5-log reduction of *Salmonella*.

After the food is pasteurized – received a 6.5-log reduction of *Salmonella* – there are still the spore pathogens, specifically, *Clostridium perfringens, Bacillus cereus,* and *Clostridium botulinum,* which are not destroyed by pasteurization but, rather, have been activated. So when the hot food begins to cool and gets below 130°F/54°C, spores can germinate and grow out. Cooling from 135°F/57°C to 41°F/5°C in 6 hours (FDA Food Code cooling) assures that there is no spore germination.

Temperature probe with remote display for the most accurate temperature monitoring.

Since most sous vide products are thin, cooling is not a significant risk. Pasteurization is the critical control. The only way one can know that proper times and temperatures have been met is to measure food temperature, which is done with a needle / thin-tipped thermocouple probe that penetrates the pouch. First, a piece of sealing foam tape, specially designed to aid in the temperature measurement of sous vide products, is placed on the pouch and then the needle probe is directed through the tape, punctures the pouch, and is inserted into the center of the food to measure its center temperature. It is crucial to ensure that consumers of the food will not become ill due to *Salmonella, E. coli* or other vegetative pathogens. Therefore, the food must get an adequate dose of heat and time to reduce the vegetative pathogens by 6.5-log, which is further complicated by trying to take the center temperature of the meat, fish or poultry.

Why, then, are there so few problems? First of all, meats being cooked by sous vide are usually from inside cuts of meat (e.g., steaks), fish and poultry, which are protected during the slaughter process and do not contain 100,000 pathogens per gram, as an outside cut (e.g., brisket, flank) would contain. The surface of these inside cuts contains fewer pathogens, and their center is virtually pathogen free. These inside cuts would have, for instance, 10 pathogens per gram. Therefore, there are not many organisms to kill. In terms of safe cooking time at 130°F/54°C, 20 minutes is probably adequate, even though the regulations require 112 minutes for a 6.5-log *Salmonella* reduction at 130°F/54°C.

Also inherent to the sous vide process is the length of time (e.g., 2 to 4 hours) in order to get the desired tenderness that the cook wants to achieve. If there are foods that do contain high pathogen counts, any surface treatment would kill most of the vegetative pathogens because the center does not have high levels of pathogens. An exception would be cooking a ground product (e.g., spiced meat pâté), where the pathogens have been ground into the middle of the food before being cooked sous vide.

In summary, sous vide cooking must be done carefully and precisely to assure that government standards are met. Government standards, however, are very conservative because pathogens on typical meat, fish and poultry sous vide products are on the surface, which gets a longer cook time than the center. The sous vide process leads towards adequate times at temperatures to get sufficient reduction of pathogens to assure that no customer will become ill eating the sous vide product. Finally, the temperature of the cooked and cooled pasteurized food is critical, which should be 41°F/54°C or less to assure that the very deadly *C. Botulinum* does not germinate, multiply and produce its lethal toxin.

O. Peter Snyder, Jr., Ph.D.

Leading food-safety expert, Hospitality Institute of Technology and Management

I very much appreciate that a culinary innovator of Nathan Myhrvold's stature has allowed me to include the following charts from his groundbreaking book *Modernist Cuisine*.

These particular charts provide an excellent means of predicting the thermal conductivity of various shapes and sizes of protein portions in water. The cooking times are similar to those predicted in the PolyScience® Sous Vide Toolbox™ application.

SUGGESTED TIMES FOR COOKING MEAT AND SEAFOOD SOUS VIDE

Sous vide cooking has many benefits, but it can be hard to estimate how long it will take. We used mathematical models, calibrated by experiments in our research kitchen, to produce the tables below. They offer estimated cooking times for foods of various shapes with the water bath set 2°F / 1°C higher than the core temperature you want the food to achieve (see page 2·246 of *Modernist Cuisine*). The times are calculated for food having thermal properties typical of most meat and seafood, but they should be roughly accurate for most plant foods as well. Note that the times are approximate—because many variables are involved in the calculations, this is not an exact guide and should not be relied upon

Table 1. Cooking times for cylinder-shaped meats having a diameter of 15 cm / 6 in

ΔT (°C)	0.5	1.0	1.5	2.0	2.5	3.0	4.0	5.0	6.0	7.5	10.0	12.5	15.0	ΔT (°F)
5	3m 25s	8m 06s	14m 04s	21m 20s	29m 51s	39m 30s	1h 01m	1h 24m	1h 47m	2h 19m	3h 05m	3h 40m	4h 07m	9
10	4m 33s	10m 41s	18m 29s	27m 55s	38m 53s	51m 10s	1h 18m	1h 46m	2h 14m	2h 53m	3h 50m	4h 34m	5h 08m	18
15	5m 13s	12m 15s	21m 11s	31m 57s	44m 23s	58m 14s	1h 28m	1h 59m	2h 30m	3h 14m	4h 18m	5h 07m	5h 45m	27
20	5m 44s	13m 25s	23m 09s	34m 54s	48m 22s	1h 03m	1h 35m	2h 09m	2h 42m	3h 30m	4h 38m	5h 31m	6h 11m	36
25	6m 07s	14m 20s	24m 42s	37m 13s	51m 29s	1h 07m	1h 41m	2h 16m	2h 51m	3h 41m	4h 54m	5h 50m	6h 33m	45
30	6m 26s	15m 04s	25m 59s	39m 05s	54m 01s	1h 10m	1h 46m	2h 22m	2h 59m	3h 52m	5h 07m	6h 06m	6h 50m	54
35	6m 43s	15m 42s	27m 03s	40m 44s	56m 08s	1h 13m	1h 49m	2h 28m	3h 06m	4h 00m	5h 17m	6h 18m	7h 05m	63
40	6m 57s	16m 15s	27m 57s	42m 01s	57m 56s	1h 16m	1h 53m	2h 32m	3h 11m	4h 06m	5h 27m	6h 31m	7h 18m	72
45	7m 10s	16m 46s	28m 55s	43m 17s	59m 53s	1h 18m	1h 56m	2h 36m	3h 17m	4h 14m	5h 36m	6h 41m	7h 29m	81
50	7m 22s	17m 12s	29m 34s	44m 22s	1h 01m	1h 19m	1h 59m	2h 40m	3h 21m	4h 20m	5h 43m	6h 49m	7h 39m	90
55	7m 34s	17m 35s	30m 12s	45m 18s	1h 03m	1h 21m	2h 01m	2h 43m	3h 25m	4h 24m	5h 51m	6h 57m	7h 48m	99
60	7m 40s	17m 51s	30m 52s	46m 18s	1h 04m	1h 23m	2h 04m	2h 46m	3h 29m	4h 29m	5h 55m	7h 04m	7h 56m	108
65	7m 45s	18m 16s	31m 31s	47m 07s	1h 05m	1h 24m	2h 05m	2h 49m	3h 32m	4h 32m	6h 02m	7h 11m	8h 03m	117
70	7m 59s	18m 34s	32m 02s	48m 10s	1h 06m	1h 25m	2h 08m	2h 51m	3h 35m	4h 37m	6h 07m	7h 18m	8h 11m	126
75	8m 06s	18m 54s	32m 20s	48m 25s	1h 07m	1h 27m	2h 09m	2h 53m	3h 38m	4h 41m	6h 12m	7h 24m	8h 16m	135
80	8m 15s	19m 04s	32m 49s	49m 10s	1h 08m	1h 27m	2h 11m	2h 55m	3h 40m	4h 44m	6h 17m	7h 30m	8h 29m	144
85	8m 17s	19m 23s	33m 24s	49m 46s	1h 08m	1h 29m	2h 12m	2h 57m	3h 43m	4h 47m	6h 22m	7h 37m	8h 29m	153
90	8m 25s	19m 35s	33m 37s	50m 12s	1h 09m	1h 29m	2h 14m	3h 00m	3h 45m	4h 52m	6h 28m	7h 39m	8h 35m	162
95	8m 31s	19m 45s	33m 57s	50m 43s	1h 10m	1h 31m	2h 15m	3h 01m	3h 48m	4h 56m	6h 29m	7h 44m	8h 41m	171
100	8m 33s	19m 56s	34m 13s	51m 02s	1h 11m	1h 32m	2h 16m	3h 04m	3h 51m	4h 57m	6h 30m	7h 49m	8h 48m	180
105	8m 41s	20m 09s	34m 34s	52m 05s	1h 11m	1h 32m	2h 18m	3h 06m	3h 51m	4h 59m	6h 37m	7h 54m	8h 52m	189
110	8m 45s	20m 14s	35m 11s	52m 24s	1h 12m	1h 33m	2h 18m	3h 06m	3h 54m	5h 02m	6h 42m	7h 58m	8h 56m	198
115	8m 49s	20m 33s	35m 29s	53m 06s	1h 12m	1h 34m	2h 20m	3h 08m	3h 56m	5h 05m	6h 43m	8h 02m	9h 01m	207
120	8m 55s	20m 47s	35m 47s	53m 21s	1h 13m	1h 35m	2h 21m	3h 09m	3h 58m	5h 08m	6h 47m	8h 07m	9h 07m	216
125	9m 01s	20m 56s	35m 52s	53m 43s	1h 14m	1h 36m	2h 22m	3h 10m	4h 00m	5h 09m	6h 52m	8h 10m	9h 10m	225
130	9m 10s	21m 06s	36m 09s	54m 33s	1h 15m	1h 36m	2h 23m	3h 12m	4h 02m	5h 11m	6h 55m	8h 14m	9h 14m	234
	³⁄₁₆	⅜	⅝	¾	1	1⅛	1⅝	2	2⅜	3	4	5	6	

Thickness (in)

for critical situations. A temperature probe provides more reliable information on how close the food is to being done, but the tables can be helpful in planning. For irregularly shaped foods, use the dimensions of the thickest part.

These tables were produced using a thermal diffusivity value of 0.13mm²/s and a heat transfer coefficient of 100W/m²K. For more on these important thermodynamic parameters, see page 1·279 of *Modernist Cuisine*.

Table 2. Cooking times for cylinder-shaped meats having a length of 15 cm / 6 in

ΔT (°C)	Diameter (cm)												ΔT (°F)
	1.0	1.5	2.0	2.5	3.0	4.0	5.0	6.0	7.5	10.0	12.5	15.0	
5	3m 57s	6m 50s	10m 18s	14m 24s	19m 07s	30m 23s	44m 04s	59m 53s	1h 27m	2h 18m	3h 12m	4h 07m	9
10	5m 10s	8m 51s	13m 17s	18m 29s	24m 29s	38m 46s	56m 00s	1h 16m	1h 49m	2h 52m	3h 59m	5h 08m	18
15	5m 54s	10m 06s	15m 08s	21m 03s	27m 50s	43m 57s	1h 03m	1h 25m	2h 03m	3h 13m	4h 28m	5h 45m	27
20	6m 27s	11m 00s	16m 28s	22m 53s	30m 15s	47m 43s	1h 09m	1h 32m	2h 13m	3h 28m	4h 49m	6h 11m	36
25	6m 52s	11m 43s	17m 31s	24m 20s	32m 08s	50m 38s	1h 13m	1h 38m	2h 20m	3h 40m	5h 05m	6h 33m	45
30	7m 13s	12m 17s	18m 23s	25m 30s	33m 40s	53m 12s	1h 16m	1h 43m	2h 27m	3h 50m	5h 19m	6h 50m	54
35	7m 32s	12m 47s	19m 09s	26m 35s	35m 07s	55m 05s	1h 19m	1h 46m	2h 32m	3h 58m	5h 30m	7h 05m	63
40	7m 46s	13m 16s	19m 45s	27m 24s	36m 08s	56m 50s	1h 21m	1h 50m	2h 37m	4h 06m	5h 41m	7h 18m	72
45	7m 58s	13m 37s	20m 19s	28m 10s	37m 14s	58m 35s	1h 24m	1h 53m	2h 41m	4h 13m	5h 49m	7h 29m	81
50	8m 13s	13m 59s	20m 53s	28m 57s	38m 11s	1h 00m	1h 26m	1h 55m	2h 44m	4h 17m	5h 57m	7h 39m	90
55	8m 26s	14m 18s	21m 16s	29m 30s	38m 54s	1h 01m	1h 27m	1h 57m	2h 48m	4h 23m	6h 04m	7h 48m	99
60	8m 34s	14m 32s	21m 42s	30m 04s	39m 47s	1h 02m	1h 29m	1h 59m	2h 50m	4h 28m	6h 11m	7h 56m	108
65	8m 43s	14m 47s	22m 06s	30m 33s	40m 07s	1h 03m	1h 30m	2h 01m	2h 54m	4h 31m	6h 17m	8h 03m	117
70	8m 48s	15m 01s	22m 25s	30m 59s	40m 44s	1h 04m	1h 32m	2h 03m	2h 56m	4h 36m	6h 24m	8h 11m	126
75	8m 59s	15m 13s	22m 45s	31m 30s	41m 32s	1h 05m	1h 33m	2h 05m	2h 59m	4h 39m	6h 28m	8h 16m	135
80	9m 06s	15m 28s	23m 07s	31m 57s	42m 11s	1h 06m	1h 35m	2h 07m	3h 01m	4h 42m	6h 35m	8h 29m	144
85	9m 15s	15m 42s	23m 30s	32m 31s	42m 43s	1h 07m	1h 36m	2h 08m	3h 03m	4h 48m	6h 39m	8h 29m	153
90	9m 22s	15m 50s	23m 38s	32m 46s	43m 15s	1h 07m	1h 36m	2h 10m	3h 06m	4h 49m	6h 41m	8h 35m	162
95	9m 27s	16m 05s	23m 52s	33m 07s	43m 53s	1h 09m	1h 38m	2h 11m	3h 07m	4h 52m	6h 45m	8h 41m	171
100	9m 32s	16m 18s	24m 16s	33m 36s	44m 17s	1h 09m	1h 38m	2h 12m	3h 08m	4h 55m	6h 50m	8h 48m	180
105	9m 42s	16m 19s	24m 25s	33m 47s	44m 27s	1h 10m	1h 39m	2h 13m	3h 10m	4h 58m	6h 55m	8h 52m	189
110	9m 44s	16m 30s	24m 31s	34m 03s	44m 53s	1h 10m	1h 40m	2h 15m	3h 13m	5h 00m	6h 57m	8h 56m	198
115	9m 49s	16m 36s	24m 47s	34m 06s	45m 15s	1h 11m	1h 41m	2h 16m	3h 13m	5h 03m	7h 01m	9h 01m	207
120	9m 52s	16m 47s	25m 03s	34m 42s	45m 43s	1h 12m	1h 43m	2h 17m	3h 15m	5h 07m	7h 04m	9h 07m	216
125	10m 00s	16m 57s	25m 20s	35m 04s	46m 17s	1h 12m	1h 43m	2h 18m	3h 18m	5h 09m	7h 08m	9h 10m	225
130	10m 06s	17m 06s	25m 23s	35m 07s	46m 27s	1h 13m	1h 44m	2h 19m	3h 19m	5h 10m	7h 11m	9h 14m	234
	⅜	⅝	¾	1	1⅛	1⅝	2	2⅜	3	4	5	6	

Diameter (in)

SUGGESTED TIMES FOR COOKING MEAT AND SEAFOOD SOUS VIDE

continued

HOW TO Use the Sous Vide Tables

1 Calculate ΔT by subtracting the starting temperature of the food from the desired final temperature.

2 Choose the table that best fits the shape of the food. For disc-like foods that are roughly circular and about 15 cm / 6 in. in diameter, use table 1. For long, cylindrical foods (like sausages) that are 15 cm / 6 in or longer, use table 2. For cubes, spheres, or squat cylinders, use table 3. For slabs much longer than they are thick, use table 4.

Table 3. Cooking times for cylinder-shaped meats having thickness roughly equal to their diameter

ΔT (°C)	0.5	1.0	1.5	2.0	2.5	3.0	4.0	5.0	6.0	7.5	10.0	12.5	15.0	ΔT (°F)
5	15s	0m 58s	2m 11s	3m 53s	6m 04s	8m 45s	15m 33s	24m 17s	34m 59s	54m 39s	1h 37m	2h 32m	3h 39m	9
10	18s	1m 12s	2m 43s	4m 50s	7m 33s	10m 52s	19m 19s	30m 10s	43m 27s	1h 08m	2h 01m	3h 09m	4h 32m	18
15	20s	1m 21s	3m 03s	5m 24s	8m 27s	12m 10s	21m 38s	33m 48s	48m 40s	1h 16m	2h 15m	3h 31m	5h 04m	27
20	22s	1m 28s	3m 17s	5m 50s	9m 07s	13m 07s	23m 19s	36m 26s	52m 28s	1h 22m	2h 26m	3h 48m	5h 28m	36
25	23s	1m 33s	3m 28s	6m 10s	9m 38s	13m 53s	24m 40s	38m 32s	55m 30s	1h 27m	2h 34m	4h 01m	5h 47m	45
30	24s	1m 37s	3m 37s	6m 26s	10m 03s	14m 28s	25m 47s	40m 13s	57m 55s	1h 30m	2h 41m	4h 11m	6h 02m	54
35	25s	1m 40s	3m 45s	6m 39s	10m 24s	14m 57s	26m 38s	41m 37s	59m 56s	1h 34m	2h 46m	4h 20m	6h 15m	63
40	26s	1m 43s	3m 52s	6m 52s	10m 43s	15m 26s	27m 26s	42m 52s	1h 02m	1h 36m	2h 51m	4h 28m	6h 26m	72
45	27s	1m 46s	3m 58s	7m 03s	11m 00s	15m 51s	28m 10s	44m 02s	1h 03m	1h 39m	2h 56m	4h 35m	6h 36m	81
50	27s	1m 48s	4m 03s	7m 12s	11m 14s	16m 11s	28m 40s	44m 47s	1h 04m	1h 41m	2h 59m	4h 40m	6h 43m	90
55	28s	1m 50s	4m 08s	7m 20s	11m 28s	16m 30s	29m 23s	45m 53s	1h 06m	1h 43m	3h 04m	4h 47m	6h 53m	99
60	28s	1m 52s	4m 12s	7m 28s	11m 40s	16m 47s	29m 48s	46m 39s	1h 07m	1h 45m	3h 07m	4h 52m	7h 00m	108
65	29s	1m 54s	4m 17s	7m 37s	11m 54s	17m 07s	30m 27s	47m 33s	1h 08m	1h 48m	3h 10m	4h 57m	7h 08m	117
70	29s	1m 56s	4m 21s	7m 43s	12m 04s	17m 23s	30m 51s	48m 09s	1h 09m	1h 48m	3h 13m	5h 01m	7h 14m	126
75	29s	1m 57s	4m 24s	7m 50s	12m 13s	17m 37s	31m 21s	48m 57s	1h 10m	1h 50m	3h 16m	5h 06m	7h 20m	135
80	30s	1m 59s	4m 28s	7m 56s	12m 24s	17m 52s	31m 41s	49m 35s	1h 11m	1h 52m	3h 18m	5h 10m	7h 26m	144
85	30s	2m 00s	4m 30s	8m 00s	12m 29s	17m 59s	31m 56s	50m 04s	1h 12m	1h 53m	3h 20m	5h 12m	7h 29m	153
90	30s	2m 02s	4m 32s	8m 06s	12m 39s	18m 14s	32m 24s	50m 39s	1h 13m	1h 54m	3h 22m	5h 16m	7h 35m	162
95	31s	1m 59s	4m 36s	8m 12s	12m 48s	18m 27s	32m 44s	51m 14s	1h 14m	1h 55m	3h 25m	5h 20m	7h 41m	171
100	31s	2m 00s	4m 39s	8m 15s	12m 55s	18m 36s	33m 06s	51m 42s	1h 15m	1h 56m	3h 27m	5h 23m	7h 45m	180
105	31s	2m 05s	4m 44s	8m 22s	13m 03s	18m 51s	33m 33s	52m 24s	1h 16m	1h 58m	3h 29m	5h 27m	7h 51m	189
110	32s	2m 07s	4m 45s	8m 26s	13m 11s	18m 59s	33m 46s	52m 46s	1h 16m	1h 59m	3h 31m	5h 29m	7h 55m	198
115	32s	2m 07s	4m 46s	8m 27s	13m 14s	19m 01s	33m 50s	52m 47s	1h 16m	1h 59m	3h 31m	5h 30m	7h 55m	207
120	32s	2m 08s	4m 48s	8m 32s	13m 19s	19m 09s	34m 03s	53m 05s	1h 16m	1h 59m	3h 32m	5h 32m	7h 58m	216
125	32s	2m 09s	4m 50s	8m 37s	13m 29s	19m 21s	34m 24s	53m 47s	1h 17m	2h 01m	3h 35m	5h 36m	8h 04m	225
130	33s	2m 10s	4m 52s	8m 38s	13m 29s	19m 26s	34m 32s	53m 51s	1h 17m	2h 01m	3h 36m	5h 37m	8h 06m	234
	³⁄₁₆	⅜	⅝	¾	1	1⅛	1⅝	2	2⅜	3	4	5	6	

Thickness and diameter (in)

3 Look up the cooking time given for the ΔT you calculated and the relevant dimension of the food.

4 Cook the food in a water bath set to 1 °C / 1.8 °F above the desired final temperature, for the time given. If you want to pasteurize, you must look up pasteurization time for the desired final temperature and add this to the cooking time listed in the table.

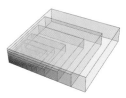

Table 4. Cooking times for slabs of meat whose width and length is at least five times the thickness

ΔT (°C)	Thickness (cm)													ΔT (°F)
	0.5	1.0	1.5	2.0	2.5	3.0	4.0	5.0	6.0	7.5	10.0	12.5	15.0	
5	40s	2m 38s	5m 56s	10m 33s	16m 30s	23m 45s	42m 13s	1h 06m	1h 35m	2h 28m	4h 24m	6h 52m	9h 54m	9
10	51s	3m 26s	7m 42s	13m 42s	21m 24s	30m 49s	54m 47s	1h 26m	2h 03m	3h 13m	5h 42m	8h 55m	12h 50m	18
15	59s	3m 55s	8m 48s	15m 39s	24m 26s	35m 14s	1h 03m	1h 38m	2h 21m	3h 40m	6h 31m	10h 12m	14h 41m	27
20	1m 04s	4m 16s	9m 35s	17m 03s	26m 38s	38m 21s	1h 08m	1h 47m	2h 33m	4h 00m	7h 06m	11h 06m	15h 59m	36
25	1m 08s	4m 33s	10m 13s	18m 09s	28m 21s	40m 49s	1h 13m	1h 53m	2h 43m	4h 15m	7h 34m	11h 49m	17h 01m	45
30	1m 12s	4m 46s	10m 44s	19m 04s	29m 48s	43m 01s	1h 16m	1h 59m	2h 52m	4h 29m	7h 58m	12h 27m	17h 56m	54
35	1m 14s	4m 58s	11m 09s	19m 49s	31m 05s	44m 47s	1h 20m	2h 04m	2h 59m	4h 40m	8h 18m	12h 57m	18h 39m	63
40	1m 17s	5m 07s	11m 32s	20m 34s	32m 08s	46m 15s	1h 22m	2h 08m	3h 05m	4h 49m	8h 34m	13h 23m	19h 16m	72
45	1m 19s	5m 16s	11m 52s	21m 05s	32m 56s	47m 26s	1h 24m	2h 12m	3h 10m	4h 56m	8h 47m	13h 44m	19h 46m	81
50	1m 21s	5m 25s	12m 12s	21m 42s	33m 56s	48m 49s	1h 27m	2h 16m	3h 15m	5h 05m	9h 03m	14h 08m	20h 21m	90
55	1m 23s	5m 31s	12m 27s	22m 06s	34m 31s	49m 45s	1h 28m	2h 18m	3h 19m	5h 11m	9h 12m	14h 23m	20h 44m	99
60	1m 25s	5m 38s	12m 40s	22m 31s	35m 10s	50m 38s	1h 30m	2h 21m	3h 23m	5h 17m	9h 23m	14h 40m	21h 06m	108
65	1m 26s	5m 45s	12m 56s	22m 58s	35m 54s	51m 40s	1h 32m	2h 23m	3h 27m	5h 23m	9h 34m	14h 57m	21h 31m	117
70	1m 28s	5m 49s	13m 11s	23m 25s	36m 35s	52m 38s	1h 34m	2h 26m	3h 31m	5h 29m	9h 45m	15h 14m	21h 56m	126
75	1m 29s	5m 56s	13m 21s	23m 42s	37m 00s	53m 15s	1h 35m	2h 28m	3h 33m	5h 34m	9h 53m	15h 27m	22h 14m	135
80	1m 30s	6m 01s	13m 33s	24m 05s	37m 37s	54m 11s	1h 36m	2h 31m	3h 37m	5h 39m	10h 03m	15h 42m	22h 34m	144
85	1m 31s	6m 06s	13m 44s	24m 25s	38m 12s	55m 02s	1h 38m	2h 33m	3h 40m	5h 44m	10h 12m	15h 54m	22h 54m	153
90	1m 32s	6m 10s	13m 53s	24m 39s	38m 34s	55m 29s	1h 39m	2h 34m	3h 42m	5h 47m	10h 16m	16h 05m	23h 08m	162
95	1m 33s	6m 13s	13m 58s	24m 50s	38m 42s	55m 41s	1h 39m	2h 35m	3h 43m	5h 48m	10h 19m	16h 08m	23h 13m	171
100	1m 35s	6m 16s	14m 08s	25m 05s	39m 10s	56m 25s	1h 40m	2h 36m	3h 46m	5h 53m	10h 26m	16h 20m	23h 29m	180
105	1m 35s	6m 21s	14m 18s	25m 22s	39m 38s	57m 06s	1h 42m	2h 39m	3h 49m	5h 57m	10h 35m	16h 31m	23h 48m	189
110	1m 36s	6m 26s	14m 30s	25m 43s	40m 12s	57m 57s	1h 43m	2h 41m	3h 52m	6h 02m	10h 43m	16h 45m	24h 07m	198
115	1m 37s	6m 28s	14m 28s	25m 42s	40m 14s	57m 56s	1h 43m	2h 41m	3h 52m	6h 02m	10h 43m	16h 46m	24h 06m	207
120	1m 38s	6m 31s	14m 38s	25m 57s	40m 36s	58m 20s	1h 44m	2h 42m	3h 54m	6h 05m	10h 48m	16h 53m	24h 19m	216
125	1m 39s	6m 34s	14m 48s	26m 14s	41m 00s	59m 09s	1h 45m	2h 44m	3h 56m	6h 09m	10h 57m	17h 07m	24h 36m	225
130	1m 40s	6m 37s	14m 55s	26m 27s	41m 23s	59m 30s	1h 46m	2h 45m	3h 58m	6h 11m	11h 02m	17h 12m	24h 47m	234
	³⁄₁₆	³⁄₈	⁵⁄₈	¾	1	1⅛	1⅝	2	2⅜	3	4	5	6	
	Thickness (in)													

ACKNOWLEDGEMENTS

It may seem unusual for someone to feel indebted to a cooking method, but I can honestly say that sous vide cooking has changed my life.

Developing sous vide cooking equipment has not only made me a better cook, it has allowed me to forge lasting connections with some of the hardest-working and most creative individuals in the culinary industry.

I am grateful to these incredible professionals for all of the contributions they have made to this book, which I sincerely hope will help chefs of all skill levels find more joy and satisfaction in their own kitchens. Unfortunately, I don't have the space to acknowledge all of the people who helped make this book possible, but several names must be highlighted.

I would like to thank Jason Sayers, who was the very first employee of the PolyScience culinary team and remains an integral member of our organization today. Over the years, Jason has been instrumental in building our brand and maintaining a host of vital relationships.

I would also like to thank Karin Zarins, who fielded that first fateful phone call for sous vide equipment from chef Matthias Merges. Responding to the needs of chef Merges was the spark that launched PolyScience Culinary.

My gratitude goes out to the entire PolyScience Culinary team, both past and present, including our chef David Pietranczyk for his kitchen and recipe expertise as well as sales manager Konrad Serafin, who has continued to cultivate important relationships, while tirelessly pursuing new opportunities for this company.

Thanks to Greg Kirrish for managing this project and offering his food and beverage insight, as well as Nicoletta Eshbaugh and Adam Ristich for their support in daily operations, customer service and account management. I am also indebted to Bill Cesaroni of Cesaroni Design for helping develop our award-winning products.

I am honored that Bruno Goussault, the grandfather of sous vide cooking and one of its greatest champions, not only took the time to contribute to this book but chose to share his wonderful sous vide recipe for rack of lamb.

Equal thanks are in order to Dr. O. Peter Snyder Jr., an insightful and dedicated food scientist, who not only wrote an important essay about the safety of sous vide for this book but has helped countless chefs understand the science and chemistry behind sous vide. I am also grateful to Nathan Myhrvold, author of the Modernist Cuisine cookbook, who was kind enough to allow us to reprint one of the most useful sous vide charts ever put to paper.

Chef Johnny Iuzzini truly went beyond the call in creating a special coconut cream dessert recipe for this book as well as sharing his delicious coconut-rich take on a classic passion fruit curd.

And special thanks must be given to all the amazing chefs, restaurateurs and educators who helped imbue the following pages with their knowledge, memories and insights. I consider it a rare privilege, indeed, to have been given words of wisdom from Dave Arnold, Wylie Dufresne, Grant Achatz, Thomas Keller, Nick Kokonas, Matthias Merges, Jacques Pépin, Jean-Georges Vongerichten and the late Charlie Trotter.

But above all, I want to thank my wife, Alissa, who has always been — and always will be — my creative muse, as well as our three wonderful children, who have served nobly as taste testers for many of the recipes in this cookbook.

This project would not have been possible without their support, patience and inspiring enthusiasm.

Sincerely,

Philip Preston